1. Meditations on Mary

MEDITATIONS ON MARY

Meditations
on
MARY

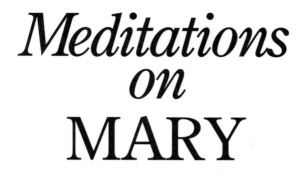

<small>Conferences by</small>

The Servant of God
TERENCE CARDINAL COOKE

Introduction by
Benedict J. Groeschel, CFR

ALBA·HOUSE alba house NEW·YORK

SOCIETY OF ST. PAUL, 2187 VICTORY BLVD., STATEN ISLAND, NEW YORK 10314

Library of Congress Cataloging-in-Publication Data

Cooke, Terence , 1921-1983.
    Meditations on Mary : conferences / by Terence Cardinal Cooke.
        p.   cm.
    ISBN 0-8189-0683-9
    1. Mary, Blessed Virgin, Saint — Meditations.   I. Title.
BT602.C64   1993
232.91 — dc20   93-26373
                                                     CIP

Produced and designed in the United States of America by the
Fathers and Brothers of the Society of St. Paul,
2187 Victory Boulevard, Staten Island, New York 10314,
as part of their communications apostolate.

ISBN: 0-8189-0683-9

Printing Information:

Current Printing - first digit   1   2   3   4   5   6   7   8   9   10

Year of Current Printing - first year shown
1993   1994   1995   1996   1997   1998

CONTENTS

INTRODUCTION

*I*n September 1958 Francis Cardinal Spellman led a pilgrimage of clergy, religious and laity to Rome, Fatima and Lourdes. The new Vice Chancellor, Msgr. Terence Cooke, accompanied Cardinal Spellman as spiritual director of this pilgrimage. Although Cardinal Spellman had led several pilgrimages, this one was special. It marked the centenary of the apparition of Our Lady to St. Bernadette at Lourdes. They set sail from New York on September 8 not knowing that Cardinal Spellman's journey would be interrupted by the illness and subsequent death of Pope Pius XII. On their return voyage Cardinal Spellman had to disembark at the Azores and return to Rome for the funeral of his friend Pope Pius and for the consistory that elected Pope John XXIII. Msgr. Cooke continued on home with the pilgrims and arrived in New York with them on October 13. None of these events are recorded in the series of meditations in this book which had been prepared by Msgr. Cooke before he left on the pilgrimage. With his customary thoroughness the young priest, who was then thirty-seven years old, had written out the entire series before the pilgrimage began. Msgr. Cooke had constructed the conferences around the centennial of Lourdes and in the first meditation describes the meaning of this very popular and beloved shrine to the pilgrims.

These meditations on various Marian themes are typical of the other writings of Cardinal Cooke and display his simplicity and very personal piety. They are important to all those interested in appreciating the spirituality of the Servant of God for two reasons. First, they are entirely his own work. In later years, when he was burdened with the responsibilities of archbishop, Cardinal Cooke frequently asked others to research topics for his sermons or to develop themes for his presentations. I know from personal experience that he always revised these "ghost-written" notes adding, subtracting and developing things to fit his own style and purpose. The meditations in this volume were not composed in this way. They are entirely the work of Terence Cooke.

Secondly, these meditations are thoroughly consistent with the piety and spirituality the Cardinal thought and lived for all his adult life. His very personal and heartfelt devotion, amounting to a filial bond with the Blessed Mother, is obvious. There is nothing abstract or intellectually objective about these writings. They are not speculative at all. Older readers, familiar with the experience of Catholic piety in the first two-thirds of our century will be completely at home with this kind of very personal devotion. Younger readers who grew up, for better or worse, with a more intellectualized piety and were less personally involved may find these meditations somewhat sentimental. To appreciate this very devout approach it is important to realize that it is the piety of the Catholic immigrants, a piety rich in faith, hope and love expressed in the most personal terms and evoking the deepest responses from the individual. Like almost all devout Christians of his time Cardinal Cooke thought and spoke of Christ and the Blessed Virgin Mary and of all the saints with the conviction that these heavenly beings personally responded to him, cared for him and expected things from him. He believed that this individual relationship with beings of the transcendent world truly existed for everyone he met even for those who did not believe at all but who might yet respond to the call of salvation. This is not to say that informed Catholics do not believe this today but they do not so frequently advert to it nor do they usually respond as fervently as those who had given them their faith.

Msgr. Cooke did his homework before he wrote these meditations. They are filled with passages and ideas from Sacred

Scripture and from the writings of the Catholic tradition. Most of the time these are not identified because the writer was not giving a theological discourse but rather meditations for a devout group of ordinary people, many of whom were on in years. For example, the meditation for September 8, "Mary and Happiness," is unquestionably based on a familiar theme in the writings of St. Augustine. Yet he is only directly cited once.

I found it most interesting to read these meditations and look for clues to the personal spirituality of Terence Cooke. He was a very private person who was, paradoxically, very outgoing. Everyone knew him and yet no one knew him. He had many deep recesses in his soul that no one knew about but he revealed these accidentally when he wrote or preached. The spiritual values of Terence Cooke flash out in many places in these meditations: his profound attraction for humility, charity, kindness and forgiveness. Anyone who personally knew the Cardinal immediately sees his optimism, his uncomplicated vision of life as a journey on which one is busy doing good, his recognition of the value of suffering courageously borne and offered as a prayer to God. In fact this series of meditations provides a spiritual background for his biography and should be read only after reading the biography (cf. *Thy Will Be Done*, Groeschel & Weber, Alba House, 1990). The person familiar with the portrait of Cardinal Cooke will see it illuminated and come into clear focus by carefully pondering this series of meditations. In fact, the meditation on Mary's charity (October 9) is a summary of the personal philosophy of Terence Cooke.

The joyous personality of Terence Cooke was in surprising contrast with the personal sufferings that life had brought to him. The early death of his mother, his aunt and his young cousins, his own decades of illness all suggest that he should have been a personality characterized by a resigned melancholy. Quite the opposite is true. He literally worked at being joyous in the face of acute suffering. The following quotation from the meditation of September 19 on Mary's Sorrow gives his secret:

There are many false ideas about suffering. There are those who falsely think that the Christian way of life glorifies suffering for its own sake. Actually, the Christian ideal is to use suffering as a means of virtue, to turn evil into good, to accept pain as an atonement offered by the mystical body in union with the suffering of Christ, its head. Suffering is not good in itself. It is indifferent. The good or evil in suffering lies in a person's attitude towards it. It may be either a blessing or a curse; it may enable a person's nature or stultify it.

The Cardinal Cooke Guild is very pleased to make these meditations available because they contain the secret of holiness of Terence Cooke. We at the Guild believe that the Cardinal may be a saint for our times. His gentle but robust piety, his loving kindness in an age marked by merciless self-seeking, his fidelity in unbelieving times, his unflinching optimism in a life of incredible challenge and persistent physical pain all make our Cardinal a model for Christians in this post-Christian world. He was a citizen of Jerusalem but able to speak to Babylon. He lived in the City of God but he worked generously in the city of this world. How did he do it? The reader will find the answers hidden in this little book.

Fr. Benedict J. Groeschel, CFR
Postulator of the Cause of
the Servant of God
Terence Cardinal Cooke

PRAYER BEFORE MEDITATION

*I*n the name of the Father and of the Son and of the Holy Spirit. Amen.

Come, Holy Spirit, fill the hearts of the faithful, and kindle in them the fire of your love.

Blessed be the holy and undivided Trinity, now and forever. Amen.

Most holy and adorable Trinity, one God in three persons, I believe that you are here present; I adore you with the deepest humility, and render to you, with my whole heart, the homage which is due to your sovereign majesty.

In you I live and move and have my being. I can do nothing by my own strength, but with your grace I can do all things in accordance with your divine will.

Our Lady of Lourdes, Queen conceived without original sin, loving Mediatrix of Grace and solicitous Mother of Good Counsel, assist me in this meditation.

St. Joseph, lover and master of prayer and life in God, teach me how to pray and to walk with God. O glorious St. Joseph be with me now and at the hour of my death, so that I may die like you, embraced by Jesus and Mary.

My Guardian angel and all you angels and saints of heaven, pray and intercede for me.

Direct, O Lord, we beseech you, all our actions by your inspiration and carry them on by your assistance that every prayer and work of ours may begin always from you and through you be happily concluded. Amen.

THE NEVER-ENDING MIRACLE OF LOURDES

SEPTEMBER 8TH
Feast of the Birthday of the Blessed Virgin Mary

"Heeding your voice, O Immaculate Virgin of Lourdes, we hasten to your feet at the humble grotto where you deigned to appear to show the way of prayer and penitence to those astray, and to dispense to the stricken the graces and wonders of your unsurpassed kindness." These words are taken from the pilgrimage prayer composed by Our Holy Father, Pope Pius XII — which we shall be reciting together each day during our journey.

1. This afternoon it is our privilege to begin our pilgrimage to Lourdes under the leadership of His Eminence on the Birthday of the Blessed Virgin Mary. As you know today is the anniversary of our Cardinal's episcopal consecration and so we rejoice with him and thank almighty God for the opportunity of being associated with him on this voyage.

We have set sail on this feast of Our Lady to experience the never-ending miracle of Lourdes. Lourdes, which in 100 years has risen from the obscurity of a tiny mountain village to one of the centers of the Church's devotion, might be called "the city that Our Lady built."

The Blessed Virgin herself started the tremendous development of Lourdes and its surroundings when, during her 11th apparition to St. Bernadette, she said, "Go and tell the priests to have a chapel built here." Later, during her 13th apparition, she told the little girl saint that she wanted the people to come to the grotto in procession.

That was in 1858 and Lourdes, hidden in the Pyrenees, was unattractive and uninspiring, with nothing more than an outdated castle used as a munitions depot, to give it outside interest.

Lourdes has become what is perhaps the greatest Christian shrine to Our Lady. Thousands of pilgrims come every year from every part of the earth to seek physical cures and spiritual graces, or simply to render homage to the Mother of God.

2. Marie Bernarde Soubirous was 14 years old on that day 100 years ago when she and her sister and their cousin went out to gather wood along the River Gave. Bernadette, as she was called in the local dialect, had always been a sickly child and was allowed to wear what, in ordinary circumstances, would have been a luxury for a girl from a family as poor as hers — woolen stockings.

When the girls got to the canal leading from the river, Bernadette decided not to cross it as much from fear of slipping into the icy water and perhaps bringing on another of her choking asthmatic attacks, as from apprehension of what her mother would say if she should get her expensive stockings wet.

Her two companions waded across the shallow stream and Bernadette stayed on the shore, close to a grotto the waters had carved from the rocks. Finally, she became lonely and felt "left out." She decided to risk crossing the canal, but first decided she would take off her precious stockings.

"I had hardly begun to take off my stockings," she said later, "when I heard the sound of wind, as in a storm.... I looked up and saw a cluster of branches and brambles.... Behind these brambles and within the opening (in the grotto) I saw immediately afterwards a girl in white, no bigger than myself, who greeted me with a slight bow of her head.... She was wearing a white dress reaching to her feet, of which only the toes appeared. The dress was gathered very high at the neck by a hem from which hung a white cord. A white veil covered her head and came down over her shoulders and arms almost to the bottom of her dress. On each foot I saw a yellow rose. The sash of the dress was blue, and hung down below her knees."

This was the first of 18 apparitions of the Blessed Mother that Bernadette was to have. Later, when asked to describe the quality of the color and material with which Our Lady's dress was made, she was shown some very fine material by a merchant. When she answered that Our Lady's dress had seemed to her to be made of much finer stuff, he responded that it would be impossible to get anything finer in all of France.

"All of which goes to show," she answered, "that the Lady did not have her dress made by you!"

People and the clergy of Lourdes were at first more than a little skeptical about Bernadette's claims that she had seen "a beautiful Lady."

On February 25, 1858, however, the Lady told Bernadette to "Go, drink at the spring and wash in it" where there was no spring. The girl scratched at the damp ground and thus began the miraculous springs from which more than 20,000 gallons of water flow each day and in which, during the past 100 years, more than 7,000 scientifically unexplainable cures have occurred.

Church authorities have never claimed that it was a new spring which was created at Lourdes, but simply that Bernadette, at the direction of Our Lady, discovered an already existing spring through which God wished to work wonders. After the discovery of the spring, the crowds coming to the grotto became larger and larger.

A striking feature of Our Lady's apparitions to Bernadette is the fact that they occurred four years after the definition of the dogma of the Immaculate Conception by Pope Pius IX was announced. Bernadette may have heard the local priest explain the doctrine at the time of the definition, but it is unlikely that she, an uneducated girl from a small mountain town, would have understood much of what he said.

After many importunities from local ecclesiastical and civil officials, Bernadette finally asked the Lady, on March 25, 1858, to tell her name. Three times she repeated, "Madame, will you be so kind as to tell me who you are?"

The Lady, she said, just smiled at her the first two times, but then after she had repeated the question once more, the apparition opened her arms and lowered them as though to include the whole world. Then she joined her hands and brought them close to her breast, Bernadette said, and raising her eyes to heaven she answered in the local dialect, "Que soy era Immaculada Concepciou — I am the Immaculate Conception."

Bernadette had to repeat these words all the way home and to the local rectory, for fear she would forget them. Later, when she was asked if she knew what they meant, she replied that she did not, but merely repeated them because that was the answer the Lady had given to her question.

The last apparition took place on July 16, 1858. There had been a three months interval between it and the preceding apparition, and Bernadette later said that she had felt she must return to the grotto that morning, during her thanksgiving after Holy Communion.

Our Lady did not say anything that last time, but only smiled and nodded her head in greeting. "Never had I seen her looking so beautiful," Bernadette said.

Bernadette joined the Sisters of Charity and Christian Instruction of Nevers in 1866. She lived a life of physical suffering and tried always to impress upon the many people who came to the convent to see her that the important fact was not that she had had the visions, but that Our Lady had shown herself to mankind.

She died in 1879 and was beatified in 1925. She was declared a saint in 1933, on December 8 — the Feast of the Immaculate Conception.

3. The question about Lourdes which mystified the late

Fulton Oursler and eventually led to his trip to Lourdes and his little book, *The Happy Grotto*, is a question that has intrigued many others. "What is the greatest miracle of Lourdes?" he once asked the Jesuit, Father McGarry. And the Jesuit answered unhesitatingly, "That's easy. It is of course, the look of resignation on the faces of those who are not healed."

Oursler went to Paris. He interviewed two of these who had not been healed. One was a lawyer named Paul Galland, who was gradually turning to stone.

The other was a young girl whose once pretty features were fast disappearing behind a hideous fungus-like growth that had already spread over three-quarters of her face. Her name was Paulette Nardeaux.

Both had been to Lourdes. And to the visiting journalist's observation that their prayers at Lourdes had not been answered, both had almost the identical reply. The lawyer said, "After I got to Lourdes, I changed my mind about praying for recovery. It is a very hard thing to explain but very easy to experience. You get on the train and are surrounded by all kinds of people young, old, babies, blind, lame — and you begin to have a conscience about your prayers.

"Those who can walk often visit during the night from one compartment to another. In an overnight ride, you get to know a lot of citizens that way. Before we were half way down the line, I had met six persons — and I hoped with all my heart that they would get well. I wanted their restoration quite as much as I wanted to be helped myself. Six to one — that is a great percentage. I felt defeated. So I prayed for my new friends and left myself out of it. And then I came back home."

The girl said to Oursler, "Monsieur, I did not pray to be healed.... There was a sick lady in the compartment next to mine. She was dying of tuberculosis. At first I prayed all the time for myself, but this little lady had many children to pray for, for she was their sole support, a charwoman in the Hotel de Ville. It came to me then how things really were. I had nobody; no family. My mother ran away. So did my father. I've always been alone. If I die, no one is hurt. So...."

The journalist asked whether the widow had been cured. "I don't know, the girl answered. I never saw her again. I only know about myself.... I feel that everything is all right with me since I visited the Happy Grotto."

Were these two stories rare, they would be edifying but not particularly significant. The fact of the matter is, however, that such stories are not rare. Indeed, this wonderful resignation to the will of God, this joy and peace and feeling of pity and beneficence is more properly a part of the atmosphere of Lourdes than even the cures are. To us who have faith in the power of God and the all-powerful intercession of the Blessed Mother, the authenticated cases of healed lungs and re-created bones are certainly marvels.

But in the long run, all these transformations of the bodies do not astound us half so much as the changes that take place — with few exceptions — in the minds and hearts of all. A man like Fred Snite makes a trip from Chicago to Lourdes in an iron lung. He has his heart set on being cured. He is young. He is wealthy. He has everything to live for. If only the Mother of God will cure him. But after a week at the grotto, he goes home again — in his iron lung. You would expect him to be bitter. You would expect that at least he would be critical. But he is not. A year later his little daughter is born and with grateful remembrance of Lourdes he calls her, Bernadette.

4. What is the secret behind this never-ending miracle? It is the power of God, of course, working through the intercession of the Blessed Virgin. There is no mystery about that as far as we are concerned. But there is a further question which opens the door to some interesting speculation. Just what does God do to the individual soul to lift it so completely out of the narrow streets of its own peculiar interests and send it hurrying off to be solicitous about others? No one can say for certain. No one can say that the answer is the same in all instances. But it seems to me that in some cases at least, God effects this wonderful result by a new and startling growth of charity in the individual soul.

Speaking to Fulton Oursler, the bedridden lawyer of Paris said that his change of heart was difficult to explain. Could it be that by retracting his steps, he might find the words he was looking for? Here he was at the Grotto of Lourdes, Paul Galland, one of the top men in his class at the Sorbonne, Doctor of Law, Diplomate of Social Sciences, Junior partner of a thriving law firm, married and the proud father of a baby boy... and a hopeless cripple, turning slowly but inexorably to solid bone. At this earlier period in his life he is still able to walk and so he does not ride a wheelchair. He is not carried in a litter. But he sits quietly on a bench behind the long rows of cots and wheelchairs at the foot of the esplanade. It is three o'clock in the afternoon. The vast throng is singing "Lauda Sion Salvatorem" and the procession of the Blessed Sacrament has begun.

During his trip from the capital with the hundreds of sick and afflicted and here at the grotto all morning long, he has watched the patience of the nurses and doctors and stretcher-bearers. He has noted the considerations of the patients one for another. In the back of his mind, no thought has been so frequent as that of charity. At Lourdes, Paul learned that if there is no conformity to the will of God there is no love. "Not my will but Thine be done." For one brief moment the thought of what this prayer involves staggers him — a trip back to Paris, eventual confinement to bed, inactivity and death. But his spirits are rallied by the sight of Our Lady's statue in the center of the domain, and beyond that the statue of little Bernadette, seemingly frozen in an eternal attitude of childlike wonder at what has come to pass at Lourdes. Mary's message for Paul Galland is a message of confidence. She herself has followed the lead of her Divine Son to glory and like him she knows over how many bridges of sorrow the road of love runs. And lest he thinks that she, like her Divine Son, is far too high above him for encouragement, she reminds him of what she did for little Bernadette herself. No potter ever began with less promising clay than Bernadette — destitute, uneducated, tubercular — yet look how she had learned to love God with her whole heart, and her whole soul, and her whole mind and all her strength.

9

5. O Immaculate Virgin of Lourdes as we hasten to your feet at the humble grotto, teach us to love God more and more. May your joy beam on our countenances. May your peace reign in our hearts. May we learn your way of prayer and penitence, your patience in suffering and your kindness and concern for others. Our Lady of Lourdes, Happy Birthday! Pray for us!

MARY AND HAPPINESS

I. Introductory Prayer: Presence of God.

II. Text

During this pilgrimage we pray to Our Lady of Lourdes with Our Holy Father, "Grant that all of us, your sons and daughters, comforted by you in our sorrows, protected in our danger, and aided in our struggles, may love and serve your gentle Jesus, and merit eternal happiness near your heavenly throne."

III. Setting

In participating in this Lourdes Centennial Pilgrimage we are joining with millions of Christians who have sought happiness following God and finding him in his sacred places. The idea of a pilgrimage is as old as the Church. The Israelites before the coming of Christ used to "go up to Jerusalem" at great festivals, walking in long files and chanting psalms. Early Christians braved all kinds of difficulties to visit the shrines of St. Peter and St. Paul in Rome. As early as the 4th century pilgrims visited the Holy Land

11

and the Holy Places, neither the barbarians nor the power of Islam was able to prevent the fulfillment of this urge. It is recorded that during the first Holy Year, Rome was visited by more than 2,000,000 people. God was the end of all these pilgrimages. The cure of an infirmity, the atonement of some fault, the fulfillment of a sacramental penance and the expression of faith were among the stirring motives of the pilgrims. In days gone by, prelates and princes, craftsmen and laborers, young and old went on difficult journeys to pray at holy shrines and to find happiness. In like manner during the past 100 years, thousands of pilgrims have found at Lourdes — Mary and happiness.

IV. Petition

O Mary, "Grant that all of us, your sons and daughters, comforted by you in our sorrows, protected in our danger and aided in our struggles, may love and serve your gentle Jesus, and merit eternal happiness near your heavenly throne."

V. Points of Meditation

1. It is difficult to find a needle in a haystack. The search for happiness is a search for something almost as difficult to find as the proverbial needle in a haystack. It goes without saying, that if we were to look for happiness in the wrong place, in a place where there actually was no happiness to be found, our search would be in vain.

All persons, without exception, desire happiness. They desire it so strongly that they constantly and diligently search for it. If they fail in their quest for happiness, it is either because they seek it where it does not exist or, while seeking it in the right place, they do not search long enough, or hard enough or in the right manner.

Something in the very nature of human beings causes them to desire happiness ardently. Something in that very nature drives them on relentlessly in their quest for happiness. Color satisfies the eye. Melodious sound fulfills the needs of the ear. Knowledge answers for the longing of the mind. Love soothes and quiets the yearning in the will. But happiness, and only happiness, can satisfy the whole person.

In her desire to be happy, Mary was no different from the ordinary man or woman. But Mary had one advantage over the average person. She was convinced that God and only God could make her completely and perfectly happy. In a degree far higher than that of any saint, she realized that nothing created, nothing material, could give her lasting happiness. On her part, no precious time was lost seeking for happiness where it did not exist. For her the search for happiness was a search for God.

The goods of this world she did not despise. Coming as they did from the creative hand of God, they could not help being good in themselves. Whether they were good for her would depend on their capacity to lead her closer to God. Each thing would have a greater or a lesser value in proportion as it led her more quickly or more surely to the ultimate possession of God.

Only in heaven would Mary be able to enjoy complete and perfect happiness. There she would see God, possess him, and enjoy the happiness of that vision and possession for all eternity. Here on earth her life is not without a high degree of bliss. To see God in this world by the light of faith is immeasurably less than to see him in heaven by the light of glory. The light of a candle cannot be compared to the light of the sun. Yet for all that, it is light and one can see by it, even though imperfectly. Each act of virtue made the light of faith stronger and clearer.

For Mary, the search for happiness was a search for God. It was a search to know him better, to love him more, and to serve him with perfect fidelity. When Jesus remained in Jerusalem to question the Doctors of the Temple, Mary had an experience similar to that of losing God. It was her only experience in searching for God and wondering whether she was searching in the right place and in the right way.

3. All persons desire happiness. Comparatively few stop to ask themselves what it is, where it can be found, and how it must be sought. The great majority assume that it is some one thing which they lack, and its absence causes pain or inconvenience. For the sick man, to find health will be to find happiness. He overlooks the fact that all healthy men are not perfectly content and happy. Poor persons, suffering from poverty, will often associate happiness with wealth. Yet if they were interchangeable words of the same meaning, how can we explain the mystery of a millionaire who is unhappy? A weak individual may confuse power with happiness. One who suffers scorn and contempt is apt to consider honor, reputation, and fame essential to happiness. All these people will waste much time seeking for the needle of happiness in the wrong haystack.

Our faith tells us, without effort on our part, what true happiness is, and where and how it can be found. Only in God, only in the knowledge, love, and possession of God, can we find complete and perfect happiness. Speaking of God, and at the same time to him, St. Augustine says, "You have made us for yourself, and our hearts are restless, until they rest in you."

Our soul has a capacity for the Infinite. Nothing finite, nothing limited, nothing temporal, nothing which grows old, decays, and corrupts, nothing in any way imperfect, will ever satisfy our soul. God, and God alone, and no one but God, can ever completely satisfy our soul.

Even in the search for God there is a certain satisfaction, a certain limited degree of happiness. For as long as we are actually searching for him, we are to some extent, in a faint degree, finding him.

How do we carry on this search? First, we try to learn all that we can about God. But knowledge, even about God, is not an end in itself. In this life it is a means to an end. The searcher wants to

14

know him better that he may serve more faithfully and love more intensely. That is his end. "Every new thing known about God is a new reason for loving him.... It would be a strange God who could be loved better by being known less" (Sheed, *Theology and Sanity*, p. 10). With the prayer of St. Augustine on our lips we have nothing to fear: "O Lord Jesus, let me know myself, let me know you and desire nothing."

VI. Thought for the Day

"Here I am, O Lord, for you have called me" (1 Samuel 3:6). With these words Samuel answered the Lord and these words express our spirit at this time. Our pilgrimage is a time of prayer and of exceptional grace. It is an adventure into the unknown. It may yield experiences that can have a decisive effect on the eternal destiny of our souls. Our pilgrimage is a miniature of life and so the purpose of this pilgrimage is the purpose of life: through Mary, to know Christ better is to love him more; to love him more inevitably results in perfect service and happiness.

VII. Concluding Prayer

"Memorare."

MARY'S CHARITY

I. Introductory Prayer

II. Text

"Let all that you do be done in charity." These are the words of St. Paul as found in his First Epistle to the Corinthians (16:14).

III. Setting

As a background and a setting for our meditation this morning, I suggest that we recall our favorite picture or statue of the Blessed Mother with the Infant Savior in her arms. This picture or statue reminds us that the purpose of life is to love and to be loved — to give ourselves to God and to give God to others.

IV. Petition

The fruit that we ask for is that all that we do will be done in charity.

V. Points of Meditation

Our Lord said "I have come to cast fire on the earth and what would I but that it be enkindled."

1. God who is love came on earth to enkindle in the hearts of all the flame of his divine love but in no heart did he enkindle so much love as in the heart of his Blessed Mother. Her heart was entirely pure from all earthly affections, and fully prepared to burn with this blessed flame. The heart of Mary became all fire and flames, as we read of her in the Book of Canticles, "The lamps thereof are fire and flame." St. Anselm explains this as fire burning within through love and flames shining without by the example that she gave to all in the practice of virtues (Ap. Corn. a Lap.). When the Blessed Virgin Mary was in this world and bore Jesus in her arms, she could well be called "fire carrying fire." The Holy Ghost heated, inflamed and melted Mary with love as fire does iron — so that the flame of the Holy Spirit was seen and nothing was felt but the fire of the love of God. St. Bernard says, "Divine love so penetrated and filled the soul of Mary, that no part of her was left untouched; so that she loved with her whole heart, with her whole soul, with her whole strength, and was full of grace" (*In. Cant.* s. 29). St. Bernardine exclaims, "Behold the power of the Virgin Mother: she wounded and took captive the heart of God" (*Pro Fest V.M.* S. 5, C. 4).

Since our Blessed Mother loves God so much, there can be nothing that she requires more of her followers than that they should also love God to their utmost. And, because Mary was all on fire with the love of God, all who love and approach her are inflamed with this same love because as a true mother she makes them like herself.

The true charity that we are considering this morning is an infused virtue by which we love God for his own sake and above all things and our neighbor as ourselves for the love of God. It is infused because we obtain it only if God is pleased to pour it into our souls. It is the best gift that God can give us. It is the end, the aim, the perfection, the crown of the Christian life. If we possess it we have all things — without it we are nothing. "If I speak with the tongues of men and of angels but do not have charity, I have become as sounding brass or tinkling symbol..." (1 Cor 13:1).

Our fervent prayer is that this pilgrimage to Lourdes will be a journey of love spent in union with Our Lord and his Blessed Mother.

2. Charity embraces in its loving clasp not only God, but also our neighbor. To love all people with a true love, to desire their well-being, to succor them in their need, to console them in their afflictions, to bear with their defects: such are the secondary effects of the queen of all the virtues — Christian charity. "And this commandment we have from him, that he who loves God should love his brother also" (1 Jn 4:21). St. Thomas Aquinas tells us that the reason for this is that he who loves God loves all that God loves (2.2, q. 25, a. 1).

So great was Mary's charity while she was on earth that she helped the needy without ever being asked. For example, at the marriage feast of Cana she told her Son about the family's distress, "They have no wine" (Jn 2:3). She asked him to work a miracle. With what speed did she fly when there was a question of relieving her neighbor! When she went to the house of Elizabeth to fulfill an office of charity, "Mary arose and went with haste into the hill country to a town of Judah" (Lk 1:39). However, she could not have more fully displayed the greatness of her charity than she did in the offering which she made of her Son to death for our salvation. In the gospel of St. John (3:16) we read, "God so loved the world as to give his only begotten Son." St. Bonaventure says, "So also, we can say of Mary, that she so loved us as to give her only begotten Son for us."

Today, in the age of Mary in which we live, we have many evidences of her continuing charity towards us. Not least among these are the physical and spiritual gifts that have come from her charitable hands during the past one hundred years at her Shrine of Lourdes.

"There is nothing by which we can with greater certainty gain the affection of Mary than by charity towards our neighbor" (St. Gregory Nazianzen). On this pilgrimage, Mary seems to say to each and every one of us, "Be charitable as your Mother also is charitable." We may be certain that our charity towards our neighbor will be the measure of that which God and Mary will show to us. "Give and it shall be given to you... For with what measure you measure, it shall be measured to you" (Lk 4:38). St. John Chrysostom has well said, "He who assists the needy makes God his debtor" (*De Poenit.* Hom. 5).

3. "Let all that you do be done in charity." During this pilgrimage, we have wonderful opportunities to grow in our love of God and love of neighbor. For example, we are able to make frequent visits to the Blessed Sacrament, and speak to Our Lord as Our Blessed Mother did. We may speak to him in our own words, as a friend speaks to a friend, asking him to increase our charity. As we offer the Holy Sacrifice of the Mass each morning and receive Holy Communion we are drawn closer to all our fellowmen and women in the bonds of charity. Just as those who dine together become more friendly and affable toward one another, so those who partake of the same Body and Blood of Jesus Christ are imbued with a spirit of Christian charity in word and deed towards their neighbors. St. Paul tells us, "We, though many, are one body, all of us who partake of the one bread" (1 Cor 10:17). Actually when we receive Christ in Holy Communion we pledge to give him to all with whom we come in contact.

VI. Thought for the Day

Our prayer this morning is that we may continue to grow in the more excellent way of Christian charity realizing that there is no limit to Christian charity. St. Bernard says, "The measure of loving God is to love without measure."

Our Lady of Charity, pray for us.

VII.   Concluding Prayer

"Memorare."

MARY'S FAITH

I. Introductory Prayer

II. Text

"And blessed is she who has believed because the things promised to her by the Lord shall be accomplished," these words of St. Elizabeth spoken to the Blessed Virgin Mary at the time of the Visitation are recorded in the Gospel of St. Luke (1:45).

III. Setting

The scene of our meditation this morning is the Annunciation. St. Luke describes it for us: "The angel Gabriel was sent from God to a town of Galilee called Nazareth, to a virgin betrothed to a man named Joseph of the house of David, and the virgin's name was Mary. And when the angel had come to her, he said, 'Hail, full of grace, the Lord is with you. Blessed are you among women'" (Lk 1:26-28). The angel's message was to ask the consent and cooperation of the Virgin Mary in the great mystery of divine power and mercy. No scene so momentous had occurred since Eve consented to the tempter in the garden of Eden. And, until Our Lord

21

first spoke, no word so meritorious, so full of promise of joy was pronounced by any human being than Mary's act of faith, "Be it done unto me according to your word" (Lk 1:38).

IV. Petition

We ask Our Lady to give us a living faith that shows us Jesus in everything and everywhere.

V. Points of Meditation

1. Mary's faith was the most perfect that ever existed and it is most worthy of our admiration and imitation. In speaking about Our Lady's faith, we might mention that we do not find the virtue of faith in the soul of Our Divine Lord, for faith is "the evidence of things we see not" and the human soul of Christ ever beheld the beatific vision of the Divine Essence. Preeminence in the exercise of the virtue of faith belongs to Mary who, for this reason is called in the Litany of Loreto the Queen of Confessors. Those whose lives are spent in disseminating in one way or another the Gospel of Jesus Christ, take Mary for their patroness.

St. Irenaeus says, "The evil done by Eve's incredulity was remedied by Mary's faith" (*Adv. Haeres.* I. 3, c. 33). Eve, contrary to the assurance she had received from God, believed the serpent and brought death into the world. Mary, Our Queen, believed the angel when he told her that she, remaining a virgin, would become the Mother of God and in this way, she brought salvation into the world. St. Augustine says, that when Mary consented to the Incarnation of the Eternal Word, by means of her faith she opened heaven to men" (Spinelli, *M. Deip.* C. 21, n. 7).

What tremendous demands were made on Mary's faith! In the beautiful words of St. Alphonsus: "The most Holy Virgin had more faith then all men and angels. She saw her Son in the crib of

Bethlehem, and believed him the Creator of the world. She saw him fly from Herod, and yet believed him the King of kings. She saw him born and believed him eternal. She saw him poor and in need of food, and believed him the Lord of the universe. She saw him lying on straw, and believed him omnipotent. She observed that he did not speak, and she believed him Infinite Wisdom. She heard him weep, and believed him the Joy of Paradise. In fine, she saw him in death, despised and crucified, and, although faith wavered in others, Mary remained firm in the belief that he was God" (*The Glories of Mary*, Part IV, p. 565). "And blessed is she who has believed, because the things promised to her by the Lord shall be accomplished."

2. Faith is the root and basis of our justification. It is a supernatural gift which God bestows upon the soul, to guide it toward the possession of his love upon earth and of himself in heaven. By the theological virtue of faith, our intellect believes the truths of revelation, Although it does not comprehend them, it nevertheless assents to them freely, but at the same time most firmly as though these truths were made evident to it. Faith also keeps us from error, and holds always before our eyes the last end for which we were created, thus guiding our steps in the way of salvation.

Faith is a priceless gift and it is the foundation of the whole supernatural life. It is the first thing that Our Lord demands of all who wish to follow him. "Only have faith," he said to Jairus, the ruler of the synagogue, about his daughter, "and she shall be saved" (Lk 8:50). To the blind men, who implored the exercise of his healing power, he said, "According to your faith be it done unto you." To a lively faith, Jesus can refuse nothing. The Canaanite woman heard the comforting words, "O woman, great is your faith! Let it be done as you wish" (Mt 15:28).

For us, faith means accepting Christ without reserve — accepting his works, his Church and his Sacraments. It means accepting the whole plan of Divine Providence and seeing in Jesus Christ the beginning and end of all things.

3. As we strive to imitate Mary's faith, we must remember that faith is not only a gift but also a virtue. It is a gift of God since it is a light infused by him into our souls. It is a virtue since the soul has to exercise itself in the practice of it. Faith is a rule of our belief and a guide of our actions. If we really believe, we should put into practice what we believe. St. James declares, "Faith without works is dead" (Jm 2:26).

While I am making this pilgrimage to Lourdes, this journey of faith to the shrine of Our Blessed Mother, I might ask myself some questions. Am I deeply attached to my Catholic Faith? Do I esteem it above all earthly treasures? Do I keep it secure from the doubts and dangers of unbelief and impiety? What means do I use to increase my knowledge of it? Do I seek to impart it to others? I believe, indeed, God's revealed truth, but is my conduct in keeping with my profession? I believe that God is everywhere, sees all, hears all and yet I sin! I believe in heaven as the reward of the virtuous and in hell as the punishment of sinners, and yet I sin! I believe that I am made for eternity, yet I live chiefly for the things of time! I believe that in prayer I speak to God, yet I pray in a careless and distracted manner! I believe that Jesus is present in the Blessed Sacrament to be the food of my soul and the companion of my life, yet how often do I receive him? How often do I visit him?

There are many petitions that with the help of St. Bernadette we shall place in the hands of Our Lady of Lourdes. Possibly, the most important request that we could make is for the gift of a living faith that through Mary we may see Jesus in everything and everywhere.

VI. Thought for the Day

We beseech the Blessed Virgin Mary by the merit of her faith, to obtain a lively faith for us. By means of the light of faith, may we see Jesus Christ under the veils of the Eucharist, in our own souls, in the events of the world, and chiefly in the Church. Our Lady of Lourdes, increase our faith! Holy Mary, Model of Faith, pray for us!

VII. Concluding Prayer

"Memorare."

MARY'S HOPE

I. Introductory Prayer

II. Text

"And the Virgin's name was Mary." These words from the Gospel of St. Luke (1:28) are found in this morning's Mass.

III. Setting

During an ocean voyage, we marvel at the beauty of the stars at night and we gain new insight into one of the meanings of Our Blessed Mother's name and one of her titles — Star of the Sea. On this feast of the Holy Name of Mary, we raise our eyes to the Pole Star, to Mary, the Star of the Sea. Calling on her sweet name and guided by her unerring light, we sail safely through the troubled waters of life to the safe harbor of heaven.

IV. Petition

As we pray that we may be saved by hope in Mary, the words of St. Bernard are on our lips. "You, whosoever you are, tossed about by the gales and storms of the ocean of life, fix your gaze on the 'Star of the Sea,' who is Mary. In dangers, in difficulties, in doubts, think of Mary, call on Mary to help you. Let her name be ever on your lips, let her love be ever in your heart. If you follow her, you will never go astray. If you pray to her, you will not despair. If she bears you up, you will not fall. If she leads you, you will never weary. If she helps you, you will reach the harbor" (*De Laud V.M.*, hom. 2).

V. Points of Meditation

1. Mary is our hope during life and at death. The name of Mary, the Mother of God is filled with divine graces and blessings. St. Bonaventure says that the name of Mary "cannot be pronounced without bringing some grace to him who does so devoutly" (*Spec. B.V.,* Lect. 9). St. Ambrose declares that the sweet name of Mary "... is a precious ointment, which breathes forth the odor of divine grace" (*Instit. Virg.*, c. 13). St. Ephrem declares, "that the name of Mary is the key of the gates of heaven," (*De Laud. Dei Gen.*) in the hands of those who devoutly invoke it. On this feast day, it is most fitting that we meditate on Mary, our hope — the guide of our pilgrimage through life.

Since hope is the flower of faith, we are able to say that Mary's hope grew from her faith. As her faith was tried, so was her hope, but the measure of her hope was the measure of her faith. St. Alphonsus tells us about the excellence of Our Lady's hope.

Mary showed how great was her confidence in God when she saw that her spouse St. Joseph, not knowing the cause of her miraculous conception, was troubled and minded to put her away privately. It would have seemed that it was necessary to disclose this sacred mystery to Joseph; but no, she would not herself make known the grace which she had received. She thought that it would be better to abandon herself to Divine Providence, in the full confidence that God himself would defend her innocence and reputation. Mary again showed her confidence in God when she knew that the time for the birth of Our Lord approached and was yet driven even from the lodgings of the poor in Bethlehem, and obliged to bring forth in a stable. "And she brought forth her firstborn Son, and wrapped him in swaddling clothes, and laid him in a manger, because there was no room for them in the inn" (Lk 2:7). She did not complain but abandoned herself to God, trusting in him to come to her aid in her necessity.

The confidence of the Mother of God in Divine Providence was also shown when she received notice from St. Joseph that she must fly into Egypt. On that very night she undertook the long journey to a strange and unknown country without provisions, without money, accompanied only by her Infant Jesus, and her poor spouse.

But much more did she show her confidence when she asked of her Son the miracle of the wine at the marriage feast of Cana. When she said, "They have no wine." Jesus said to her, "What would you have me do, woman? My hour has not yet come." After this answer, which seemed to be a refusal, her confidence in the divine goodness was such that she desired the servants to do whatever her Son told them; for the favor was certain to be granted. "Do whatever he tells you" (Jn 2:35).

As we rejoice today under the name and protection of the Most Holy Virgin Mary, may we learn to hope in God as she always did, especially in the great affair of our eternal salvation. (*The Glories of Mary*, Part IV, p. 569).

Hope has been called the forgotten virtue. A large number of Catholics do not place a high esteem on hope. They forget that hope ranks among the unique trio of virtues which are called theological because they effect the union of the soul with God. Some Catholics are not completely convinced that we cannot be saved without hoping. During this meditation, it is helpful to impress on our minds that these virtues are an indissoluble trinity. All three go together. You cannot have one without the other. Hope is a theological virtue and we have an obligation to practice it. If we wish to analyze our attitude towards hope we might ask ourselves how often we confess faults against hope or examine our conscience on it.

St. Paul startles us by saying that "we are saved by hope." The basis of our hope is the almighty power, and infinite benevolence of God. We depend upon God and not on ourselves. With the aid of his grace we can do all things and grace is never lacking to a person of good will. In the midst of difficulties and temptations, it is consoling to know that the human will cooperating with grace forms a combination that cannot be overcome. It has been well said that God's grace united to man's good will constitutes a majority in any situation.

The virtue of hope which stands midway between presumption and despair is the gift that we ask of the Blessed Virgin on her name day. With her help we shall conduct our lives on the assumption that "to those who love God all things work together for good."

One common obstacle to the growth of hope is excessive self-consciousness. All of us are too sensitive to the chance of failure, the possibility of criticism and a host of petty thoughts. We need the hope — the trust of St. Bernadette whose confidence in God was unshaken despite many difficulties. It is so easy for us to become discouraged. A Retreat Master said that one who keeps looking in the mirror will find good reason to become discouraged.

One of the secrets of happy living is to fix the eyes of our minds on God — to trust in his Divine Providence. Like St. Peter, we can walk over the stormy waters of life until we become afraid. Then Jesus will say to us, "O you of little faith! Why did you doubt?" (Mt 14:31). The cultivation of the virtue of hope will depend upon what we think about, what we dream of, and what we wish for. If we think less of ourselves and fix our attention on the all-essential things of God, we shall be better able to overcome trials and temptations.

We grow in hope and in holiness by first learning to see God in all things and then later by learning to see all things in God, who is both the center and the circumference, the beginning and the end. St. Theresa advises us well when she says, "Contemplate God and be at peace." The most certain means of growing in this spirit is to visit the Blessed Sacrament and receive Holy Communion frequently. This is God's gift of hope and immortality.

VI. Thought for the Day

During this pilgrimage to Lourdes, may we be strengthened in our hope in God and his Blessed Mother. With Our Holy Father we pray, "O Mystical Rose relieve crushed souls with the heavenly fragrance of hope!" Hail, Holy Queen, our life, our sweetness and our hope."

VII. Concluding Prayer

"Memorare."

MARY'S HUMILITY

SEPTEMBER 13TH
Feast of St. John Chrysostom

I. Introductory Prayer

II. Text

In teaching about the virtue of humility, our Divine Savior said, "For everyone who exalts himself shall be humbled, but he who humbles himself shall be exalted." These words are recorded in the Gospel of St. Luke (18:14).

III. Setting

On Thursday, February 11, 1858, about midday, Bernadette Soubirous accompanied by her sister, Marie Toinette, and a companion, Jeanne Abadie, went to gather firewood on the banks of the Gave River which flows at the foot of the Pyrenees mountains near the town of Lourdes in Southern France. The three children ran along the river bank and, in front of the rock of Massabielle, Bernadette stopped to remove her shoes and stockings. Suddenly she heard a gust of wind coming from within the

31

cave. She saw nothing move, not even the stray leaves from the trees. But when she raised her head she saw in a niche in the rock, high above the ground, "a beautiful Lady dressed in white, girded with a blue sash." The lady had a pearl-white rosary on her right arm and over each bare foot rested a golden rose. Frightened at the vision, Bernadette knelt on the ground and taking her rosary from her pocket she began to pray. The Beautiful Lady joined her each time that she said the Doxology. When the rosary was finished the vision vanished. This was the first appearance of the lovely Mother of God to the humble Bernadette.

In the year 1858, Our Beautiful Lady appeared not just once but eighteen times to Bernadette. This humble peasant girl was selected by God as his instrument to awaken in the minds of millions of people throughout the world a vivid faith in his supernatural power and goodness, and to increase and propagate devotion to his Immaculate Mother Mary.

IV. Petition

Our prayer in this meditation is that like St. Bernadette we will be truly humble followers of Mary. "For everyone who exalts himself shall be humbled, but he who humbles himself shall be exalted."

V. Points of Meditation

1. Before Christianity introduced a new standard of life, humility was not regarded as a virtue. The ancient Romans recognized many virtues as praiseworthy such as fortitude, temperance, prudence and justice. They understood to a greater or lesser degree loyalty, truthfulness and love of family and friends. But humility, as Christians understand it, they would never have praised. In fact, they would have despised and spurned it. It

remained for Jesus Christ by precept, and above all by the pattern of his life to teach the beauty of sincere humility. When the Divine Master said to his disciples, "Learn from me" — not to work miracles, not to create the world out of nothing, but — "to be meek and humble of heart" (Mt 11:29), he taught a doctrine until then untaught. Yet, Mary had learned the heavenly lesson, breathed into her soul by the Spirit of God, before Christ came. St. Bernard has written "Mary pleased God by her virginity; by humility she conceived him" (*De Laudibus Mariae*, Hom. 1, 5). It is the lowliness of his chosen creature which above all wooed God and won the heart of her Creator. Her humility ravished heaven. Her humility it was which drew the Word of God from his Father's side, and led him to descend from the throne of his glory to the depths of our nothingness.

Although Mary was sinless, she was the most humble of all God's creatures. Never for an instant of her life did she fail to acknowledge that all she had, she possessed as God's free gift. In the solemn hour of the Annunciation she was pleasing to God when, at the very moment of her exaltation, she professed herself to be the servant of her Lord: "Behold the handmaid of the Lord" (Lk 1:38). Again at the Visitation, in the same spirit, she at once referred Elizabeth's magnificent words of welcome and praise not to herself but to her Creator: "My soul magnifies the Lord, and my spirit rejoices in God my Savior, because he has regarded the lowliness of his handmaid.... He who is mighty has done great things for me" (Lk 1:46-49). The humility of Our Lady is again seen during the desolation of the Passion when she shared the ignominies heaped upon her dying Son, crucified between two thieves. Always, Mary retired into the shadow — even though it was the shadow of the Cross. Yet the hand of the Most High crowned her with glory: "Whoever humbles himself shall be exalted."

2. Humility is widely misunderstood in its real essence and many mistaken ideas are held about it. Although humility is a most commonsense virtue, it is perhaps the least common virtue found among human beings. Humility is nothing more nor less than a

realization of the truth concerning ourselves and an acknowledgment of it. By humility we understand that we are creatures of God and that all the good that we possess, whether in the natural or the supernatural order, has come to us from God and from God alone. As St. Paul says, "Our sufficiency is from God" (2 Cor 3:5). And in another place he asks us, "What have you that you have not received? And if you have received it why do you boast as if you had not received it?" (1 Cor 4:7). By pride, the vice directly opposed to humility, we arrogate to ourselves the claim to glory in the gifts that have been bestowed upon us, as though we owe it in some way to ourselves.

Humility does not mean self-depreciation in comparison with others. Since we see only the externals, we are totally unable to make any such comparison at all. It does not even mean thinking oneself the worst of sinners. Neither does it mean belittling one's talents given by God, but using them in all charity to benefit others. Humility does not concern itself with the possession of worldly wealth, honors, position in society, or state of life. If any of these are possessed they should be recognized as gifts from the goodness of God. The poor man may be proud, the rich humble; it is a question solely of self and God.

Humility is strength — the strength of the divine in a human heart free of pride. Humility is truth — enabling us to see ourselves as we are. Humility gives us a sense of values — keeping us in our rightful place as creatures. Humility is wisdom and its practice brings a rich reward. "Whoever humbles himself shall be exalted." Thus it is with Our Lady and her little disciple St. Bernadette.

3. What of myself? Have I a deep conviction of my unworthiness in God's sight? Do I recognize that I have failed to correspond with grace and that I am not what I ought to be? God is Almighty. I am weak, helpless and totally dependent on him. God is the Creator. I am his creature. God is life. He is being itself. I am but dust and ashes. The only things that I can claim for my very own are my sins! Such reflections as these help to keep us humble but

we have to work at it. It is not easy to be humble. We might say that it does not come "natural" to us. We must pray increasingly for this virtue which St. Bernard says "is the foundation and guardian of virtues" (*In Nat. D.*, s. 1).

It is difficult to love self-abasement and mortification as Bernadette did, to accept misunderstandings and insults as she did without complaint, to show no anxiety for success but to leave all to God — also as she did. Yet humility brings its own reward: those who humble themselves shall be exalted.

VI. Thought for the Day

Realizing that "God resists the proud, but gives grace to the humble" (Jm 4:6), we beseech Mary to protect us under the mantle of her humility. During this pilgrimage may she obtain for us the gift of being truly humble. Holy Mary, Model of Humility, pray for us.

VII. Concluding Prayer

"Memorare."

MARY'S OBEDIENCE

SEPTEMBER 14TH
Triumph of the Cross

I. Introductory Prayer

II. Text

In the epistle read in this morning's Mass of the feast of the Exaltation of the Holy Cross, St. Paul speaks about our Divine Savior, Jesus Christ, "who humbled himself, becoming obedient to death, even to death on a cross" (Ph 2:8).

III. Setting

At Lourdes, Our Lady appeared eighteen times to her obedient child, Bernadette. In the course of the apparitions she instructed Bernadette to pray for sinners and do penance for them. In the ninth apparition Our Lady directed the child to a spot near the Grotto. Obediently, Bernadette dug in the ground at the request of Our Lady and immediately water sprang forth, which later became the famous Spring of Lourdes. In the tenth apparition, Bernadette followed the command to "kiss the earth for sinners." In the eleventh apparition, Bernadette was ordered to tell the priest of the parish that the Lady of the Grotto wished to have a chapel built at Massabielle. This directive was repeated in the fourteenth apparition, "Go and tell the priest to build a chapel here and to come here in procession." It was not easy for the gentle Bernadette to face the parish priest, the Abbe Peyramale, but she did exactly as she was told. In the sixteenth apparition, at his request, Bernadette asked the Lady if she would be so good as to tell her who she was and what was her name. Her spirit of obedience was blessed with a wonderful answer. The Lady looked to heaven, and then slowly opening her hands in a gesture of majesty and grace, she said, "I am the Immaculate Conception."

IV. Petition

The whole life of Christ on earth was a series of acts of obedience to his heavenly Father. The life of our Blessed Mother had as its center God's holy will. St. Bernadette, guided by Our Lady of Lourdes, was obedient unto death. May we, through their kind assistance, obediently follow God's will. "Thy will be done on earth as it is in heaven."

V. Points of Meditation

As we have seen in a former meditation, when the angel Gabriel came to Mary he saluted her with the reverence due to her position. Then he unfolded for her consideration God's stupendous plan and, having done so, he virtually asked her if she was willing to accept her role. God never forces his gifts on his creatures. He respects their free will. So here too, he stood back, as it were, and let Mary weigh the proposition, ask any question she wanted, and then make up her mind. Through love for obedience, Mary gave the perfect answer: "Behold the handmaid of the Lord; be it done to me according to your word" (Lk 1:38). When Mary uttered her "fiat" of obedience to God's plan, she spoke for you and for me: "Be it done to *me* according to your word." St. Irenaeus says that by her obedience Our Blessed Mother repaired the evil done by Eve's disobedience. As Eve, by her disobedience, caused her own death and that of the whole human race, so did the Virgin Mary, by her obedience, become the cause of her own salvation and that of all mankind" (*Adv. Haeres.* I. 3, c. 33).

Mary showed how willing she was to obey in all things when, to please God, she followed the orders of the Roman Emperor. She undertook the long journey to Bethlehem despite the fact that she was with child. In accordance with God's will, she brought her Divine Son into the world in a lowly stable. She again manifested her spirit of obedience, when she promptly set out on the longer and more difficult journey to Egypt. Her heroic obedience to the divine will was even more evident when she offered her Son to death on Calvary's hill.

The dynamic aspect of the life of Mary's Divine Son, Jesus Christ, was obedience. His obedience not only embraced all the acts of his life, but it was heroic and uncalculating. Jesus Christ did not please himself. In the days of his boyhood, Jesus was docile and obedient to his parents at Nazareth. During his public career, his living was essentially — an obeying. That constituted its excellence in his eyes. He told his apostles that the satisfaction of all his needs was found in the execution of God's will. "My food is to do the will of him who sent me, to accomplish his work" (Jn 4:34). "He humbled himself, becoming obedient to death, even to death on a cross."

2. St. Thomas Aquinas teaches that in practicing the virtue of obedience, we despise our own will for God's sake. Therefore, obedience is more praiseworthy than any other moral virtue which despises other goods for God's sake. In other words obedience is the greatest of the moral virtues because it inclines us to yield up the stronghold of our very individuality — namely,

our will and our liberty. When we are obedient, we make a substitution of God's will as the center of our lives rather than our own. Through obedience, a religious person becomes a perfect holocaust to Almighty God. Obedience is, for a religious person, the cross of which our Lord spoke, when he said, "If anyone wishes to come after me, let him deny himself, take up his cross and follow me" (Mt 16:24). In discussing the evangelical counsels of poverty, chastity and obedience, St. Thomas considers obedience as the most excellent. He ranks obedience first because the sacrifices that it involves are the greatest that one can offer to God.

Obedience is the root of all the virtues. All human virtue to be truly virtue must have the quality of obedience to God. Of course obedience implies a constant exercise of humility and charity. It is a source of peace, of security, and of ever increasing merit. Actually obedience simplifies life marvelously. It reduces the whole of our conduct to the observation of a single duty, that of obeying.

Even in civil life obedience is looked upon as of primary importance to the success of any undertaking. Beginning with the family, the father is ordinarily looked upon as the head of the family, whom all other members of the household must obey. In any business enterprise the manager is looked upon as the guiding spirit. When a ship such as the "Olympia" leaves port to sail the high seas, the captain is given absolute authority. When a battle is in progress, the general is given supreme command to direct the maneuvers of all the soldiers under him. These examples are in accord with the teaching of St. Paul who said, "Let every person be subject to the higher authorities; for there is no authority except from God; and those that exist have been established by God. Therefore whoever resists authority, resists the ordinance of God. And those who resist will bring judgment on themselves" (Rm 13:1).

3. As children of Mary and followers of Christ every day we must try to make our life a constant act of loving submission to God's will and to the will of those who hold God's place. Our

obedience must be rendered to Christ and to our lawful superiors who represent him. It must be full of trust and confidence in Christ's infinite love and providence. Our obedience must be such that we not only are willing to do what we are told but also we are willing to be told what we are to do.

This was the spirit of our Divine Master, Jesus Christ who "humbled himself, becoming obedient to death, even to death on a cross." This was the spirit of the Blessed Mother who stood by the cross of Jesus: "Be it done to me according to your word." This was the spirit of St. Bernadette, the chosen instrument of Our Lord and his Blessed Mother. This must also be our spirit! The virtue of obedience offers the quickest way to advance in the service of God, not only is the virtue of obedience a certain road to salvation and sanctity, but it is the only road to them.

VI. Thought for the Day

On this feast day we look forward to living the wonder of Lourdes. Possibly, one of the first things that we shall see will be the graceful spire of the Basilica's central tower which is surmounted by a cross beneath which is a crown of gilded flowers, a symbol of Our Lady's diadem. May we also please God by carrying our daily cross in a spirit of obedience. "Thy will be done on earth as it is in heaven."

VII. Concluding Prayer

"Memorare."

MARY'S ZEAL

I. Introductory Prayer

II. Text

At the Last Supper, our Lord Jesus Christ said to his zealous followers, his Apostles, "I am the vine, you are the branches. He who abides in me, and I in him, bears much fruit; for without me you can do nothing" (Jn 15:56).

III. Setting

This morning we join the friends of Christ who are gathered together after his death in the upper room praying in union with Mary, the Mother of Jesus — the Queen of the Apostles. It is fitting to surmise that during those sacred days they interspersed conversation with their prayer. There could have been only one subject of interest to them and that was the inexhaustible one that occupies us each day at prayer — "Jesus Christ, yesterday, today and the same forever." His Mother, who knew him so intimately would have been especially eloquent in recounting all that she had seen him say and do. In our prayer this morning we once more "behold our Mother" and seek her guidance in glorifying God — saving our own souls and assisting in the salvation of the souls of our neighbors.

IV. Petition

Through the powerful intercession of the Blessed Virgin Mary, the Queen of the Apostles, may we receive the urge and the capacity to work hard at holiness. May we grow day by day in the practice of the important virtue of zeal.

V. Points of Meditation

1. The holy Gospels have preserved words spoken by Our Lady on four occasions — the Annunciation, the Visitation, the Finding of the Boy Christ in the Temple, and the Marriage Feast of Cana. In these words, Mary's zeal for God's honor and glory, for her own sanctification and for the spiritual welfare of her neighbor may be seen. We have been given but five short sentences, and the "Magnificat." If we take out of the "Magnificat" two sentences, we have seven sayings or words of Mary. These words of Mary contain in themselves principles which constitute Christian perfection.

In the first word of Mary at the Annunciation we clearly see the calm, strength and self-possession of Mary's zeal. To avoid undue precipitance and to be sure of her ground she asked the angel Gabriel the question, "How shall this happen, since I do not know man?" (Lk 1:34). She asked this question with an unshaken trust in the power and promises of God.

As soon as the question was answered, the second word fell from Mary's lips, "Behold the handmaid of the Lord; be it done to me according to your word" (Lk 1:38). This is the perfect, zealous, humble, attitude of a creature who wishes to live for God alone.

At the time of the Visitation, Mary's zeal towards God was expressed in her "Magnificat": "My soul magnifies the Lord and my spirit rejoices in God my Savior" (Lk 1:46-47). She magnified the Lord by dedicating to the praise and service of God her intellect, her will and all her affections. Her spirit rejoiced in God, her Savior, because her delight was to please him in all things.

The words of Our Lady's prophecy expressed in the "Magnificat" have been gloriously fulfilled in every age and especially in this Marian age in which we live. "For, behold, henceforth all generations shall call me blessed" (Lk 1:48-49). This prophecy is fulfilled in us on this Lourdes Pilgrimage as we honor the incomparable blessedness of Our Lady at Lourdes and as we shall renew our zeal with Our Lady of Fatima. The blessedness of Mary is zealously proclaimed in all tongues by all generations, by old and young, by priests and lay people, by monks in their cloisters, by virgins rapt in prayer, by the soldier in the battlefield and by the laborer tilling the field.

For three long days, Mary and Joseph zealously searched with heavy hearts for the boy Christ. Although Our Lady accepted God's will, in her zeal to be always united with Jesus, she asked a difficult question in a reverent spirit: "Son, why have you done this to us? In sorrow your father and I have been looking for you" (Lk 2:48). This question was pleasing to God and it was answered in God's appointed manner and in his chosen time.

At the marriage feast of Cana in her zeal to help others Our Lady exercised for the first time, at least in public, her office of Advocate with her Son. When the wine ran short, the Mother of Jesus said to him, "They have no wine" (Jn 2:3). Mary's petition was a perfect prayer filled with confidence. Her advice to the servants, "Do whatever he tells you" (Jn 2:5) prepared the way for a wonderful miracle. This advice is a rule of life for the truly zealous and obedient. It is a complete summary of all Christian perfection. Do whatever my Son tells you.

2. In general, zeal means ardor and fervor in the pursuit of anything. Religious zeal means ardor and fervor in the pursuit of

the virtues. The career of holiness demands more effort than any other career in life. We need the urge and capacity to work hard at holiness. This urge is what we call the important virtue of zeal.

As creatures, zeal for God's honor and glory should be our grateful response for all his goodness to us. Created beings can do nothing to increase God's *intrinsic* glory, which is complete in and of itself, independently of all things outside of himself. But creatures can, and rational creatures should, promote God's *extrinsic* glory. Indeed, the end for which God created all things from nothing is his own honor and glory. This is why we say with the Psalmist, "The heavens show forth the glory of God, and the firmament declares the work of his hands" (Ps 18:2). Therefore, nothing can be more just and equitable — nothing can be more excellent — than zeal for the glory of God.

Next to zeal for God's glory, zeal for our own holiness, our own personal salvation is our first and greatest duty. For this reason God made us and placed us upon earth for a fixed and definite period of time. Salvation then is the most important business of our lives and the one and only work of our lives. We must work at it with the utmost diligence and care — and continually and without interruption. St. Augustine said, "He who created you without your help will not save you without your help."

Zeal is a truly heavenly thing because it is the overflowing of charity. A truly zealous person's soul is filled to the brim with love of God and his charity is poured out upon the souls of others. There is nothing greater in the sight of God, nothing more pleasing, nothing more meritorious than zeal for the souls of others. In the exercise of zeal for souls we extend and build up God's kingdom by gaining him new subjects. In this way we help to realize Our Lord's Prayer, "Thy Kingdom Come." St. Denis the Areopagite tells us "of all divine things, the most divine is to cooperate with God in the salvation of souls."

3. If we would live in union with Jesus and Mary, our lives should be lives of zeal— zeal for God's honor and glory and for our own and our neighbor's spiritual welfare. "I am the vine, you are

the branches." We may show and increase our zeal by regular and fervent daily prayer — however brief it may be; by considering our attendance at Sunday Mass, and daily Mass if possible, not as a burden but as a joy; by receiving the sacraments frequently as a privilege and not as an obligation; by preferring spiritual reading to all other types of reading; by making an effort to spread the faith to non-Catholics. We may grow in zeal by performing our daily work which God has given us as perfectly as possible. God asks us to use every moment and every opportunity to develop the talent or talents that he has given us for His honor and glory, our own sanctification and our neighbor's welfare.

Today, as we visit the famous shrine of St. James at Santiago de Compostela, may our prayer be for an increase of zeal. May we have the true zeal of the apostle St. James the Greater who, according to tradition, preached the Gospel in this land. May we have the warm zeal of those who during the Middle Ages made this pilgrimage to Compostela. May we have the stirring zeal of those who built this beautiful basilica.

VI. Thought for the Day

Our prayer for this morning is that Our Blessed Mother will help us to grow in zeal so that with her we can say, "My soul magnifies the Lord and my spirit rejoices in God my Savior." Holy Mary, Model of Zeal, pray for us.

VII. Concluding Prayer

"Memorare."

MARY'S SORROW

I. Introductory Prayer

II. Text

"To what shall I compare you? Or to what shall I liken you, O daughter of Jerusalem? To what shall I equal you that I may comfort you, O virgin daughter of Sion? For great as the sea is your destruction." In these words of the Book of Lamentations (2:13), Jeremiah seems unable to find anyone with whom he can compare our Blessed Mother, our Mother of Sorrows, especially when he considers her great sufferings at the death of her Son.

III. Setting

The setting for our reflections this morning as we begin Holy Week is at the foot of the cross with our Mother of Sorrows. In the Gospel of St. John (19:25-27), read on the Feast of the Seven Sorrows of the Blessed Virgin Mary, the death of Jesus is briefly described. "At that time there were standing by the cross of Jesus his mother and his mother's sister, Mary of Cleophas and Mary Magdalene. When Jesus, therefore, saw his mother and the

46

disciple standing by whom He loved, he said to his mother, 'Woman, behold, your son.' Then he said to the disciple, 'Behold your mother.' And from that hour the disciple took her into his home." Our Lady is near to Christ and like to Christ. She is near to Christ because she is his Mother. She is like to Christ because she is our Mother whose heart overflows with compassion for our sufferings and our miseries. In no way are this nearness and likeness to her Divine Son manifested more convincingly than in the immensity of Mary's sorrows.

IV. Petition

Our petition this morning is for the grace to accept our sorrows in life in undisturbed peace of soul by uniting our sufferings with the sufferings of Our Lord and our Mother of Sorrows.

V. Points of Meditation

1. St. Alphonsus, in speaking of the dolors of Mary describes Mary as the Queen of Martyrs because her martyrdom was longer and greater than that of all the martyrs. St. Thomas Aquinas says that "to have the glory of martyrdom, it is sufficient to exercise obedience in its highest degree, that is to say, to be obedient unto death" (2.2, q. 124, a. 3). St. Bernard tells us, "Mary was a martyr, not by the sword of the executioner, but by bitter sorrow of heart" (*De Serm. D. in Coena*, s.4). He also says, "The passion of Jesus began with his birth" and therefore Mary, in all things like unto her Son, endured her martyrdom throughout her life. With this thought in mind, we are better able to understand our text of Jeremiah, "Great as the sea is your destruction." As the sea is all bitter and salt, so also was the life of Mary, always full of bitterness at the sight of the Passion of the Redeemer, which was ever present to her mind. When Jeremiah considered the greatness of the sufferings of Mary, the Mother of Sorrows, at the death of her

Son, he was unable to find anyone with whom he could compare her, "To what shall I compare you? Or to what shall I liken you, O daughter of Jerusalem?" The heart of Mary became a mirror of the Passion of her Son — faithfully reflecting the blows, the wounds and all that Jesus suffered. St. Bonaventure remarks that "those wounds which were scattered over the Body of Our Lord were all united in the single heart of Mary" (*Stim. div. am.*, p. 1, c. 3).

Although the life of Mary, like the life of Jesus was throughout a life of sorrow, Our Holy Mother the Church singles out seven sorrows or dolors from the rest so that we can lovingly cherish and commemorate them. At the time of the presentation, Simeon, taking the Child in his arms, prophesied to Mary that the Child was set for the fall of some and the resurrection of others and that he should be a sign to be contradicted. He told Mary about sorrows to come, "And your own soul a sword shall pierce, that the thoughts of many hearts may be revealed" (Lk 2:35). In the second dolor, we see that the sword of Simeon had not waited long to pierce the soul of Mary as she fled to Egypt by night in order to protect the child from the hatred of King Herod. Another special dolor of the Blessed Virgin was when she returned to Jerusalem with Joseph. Tormented and racked by anxiety Mary and Joseph searched for three long days until they found the Boy Christ. The fourth dolor recalls to our mind that dread hour when Jesus looked upon Our Lady, and Mary gazed on the bruised and bleeding face of her Son, amidst the awful clamor on the road to Calvary. In the fifth dolor, Mary stands brokenhearted beneath the Cross of Jesus where he poured forth his Precious Blood to the last drop for our redemption. We contemplate in the sixth dolor our Mother of Sorrows after the crucifixion receiving the still, inanimate, tortured Body of her Son into her arms. In the seventh dolor, we meditate on Our Blessed Lady when she said farewell to Jesus the night of that first Good Friday. Where her treasure lay, there was Mary's heart — with Jesus in the tomb. "To what shall I compare you? Or to what shall I liken you, daughter of Jerusalem? To what shall I equal you, O virgin daughter of Sion? For great as the sea is your destruction."

2. Sorrow, our inseparable associate during this earthly pilgrimage of ours, is the consequence of the ills that befall us either from within or without. Bereavement, loss of fortune, calumny, malpractices designed against us are causes of exterior affliction. Sickness, humiliation, temptation and, above all, the thought of having offended God by sin and the danger of offending him again give rise in us to interior sufferings. It is most difficult to reconcile pain and suffering with the infinite love and goodness of God. Actually it was not part of the design of creation that pain and hardships should be the lot of man. God intended all His creatures to be happy, but the free will of man upset God's plan by disobedience in claiming to be independent of God. Original sin is the cause of pain, and man must pay the penalty which results from his choice of evil. Therefore, it was man, and not God, who made this vale of tears.

There are many false ideas about suffering. There are those who falsely think that the Christian way of life glorifies suffering for its own sake. Actually, the Christian ideal is to use suffering as a means of virtue, to turn evil into good, to accept pain as an atonement offered by the mystical body in union with the sufferings of Christ, its head. Suffering is not good in itself. It is indifferent. The good or evil in suffering lies in a person's attitude towards it. It may be either a blessing or a curse; it may enable a person's nature or stultify it. An example is found in the two criminals who suffered with our Lord. Both suffered the same torments. While one accepted his state as a just punishment and obtained a promise of future happiness, the other made his state worse than before by railing and cursing. The important question is how we take suffering. Our human nature can be purified and refined by sorrow borne in patience for the love of God.

3. If we go to Mary, Our Mother, in our hour of suffering, not only shall we receive from her consolation in our affliction, but we shall also learn by her example to value at its proper worth the personal cross with which Our Lord is pleased to visit us. There is something peculiarly personal about the cross of each one of us. For one it is mental anguish, dread of death, unreasonable fear of

sins long since forgiven. For another it is a persistent and harassing temptation, hidden perhaps from every eye, never spoken of except in the sacred tribunal. For another it might be ungovernable scruples. Or it may be physical pain, incessant headaches, sleepless nights. Whatever may be the accidental differences in our personal cross, it possesses for each one of us a sort of sacramental effect. It is designed as a vehicle of much grace to the soul if we bear it in patience and for the love of God. It will make us more gentle, tolerant, sympathetic, resigned and charitable. Each time that we assist in offering the Holy Sacrifice of the Mass, we are assisting at the same sacrifice that Mary assisted in offering at Calvary. We are reminded that the royal road of the cross, the road of daily suffering is the only road to the crown of eternal glory that God has prepared for us.

In making our pilgrimage to Lourdes and Fatima we are answering the invitation of Christ who said, "Come to me, all you who labor and are heavily burdened, and I will give you rest" (Mt 11:28). We are also accepting the invitation of Our Lady of Lourdes whose hospital at Lourdes is known as the Hospital of Our Lady of the Seven Sorrows. "Come to me, all of you who desire me, and be filled with my fruits" (Si 24:18).

VI. Thought for the Day

May we frequently meditate on the words of Our Savior, "You shall be sorrowful, but your sorrow shall be turned into joy" (Jn 16:20).

"Blessed are they who mourn, for they shall be comforted" (Mt 5:5). Holy Mary, Mother of Sorrows, Comforter of the Afflicted, pray for us.

VII. Concluding Prayer

"Memorare."

MARY'S VISITATION

I. Introductory Prayer

II. Text

"Blessed art thou among women and blessed is the fruit of thy womb" (Lk 1:42). These are the words that Elizabeth addressed to the Blessed Virgin Mary when she visited her.

III. Setting

After the Annunciation, Mary recalled what the angel had said about her cousin Elizabeth who had conceived in her old age. She decided to visit her. The trip was long and tedious. Some say it took seven days. Although it was a dangerous journey because of robbers and wild animals, it was predominantly a joyful journey. It was undertaken in springtime, when the Holy Land is gorgeously rich in nature's splendors. We can see the budding flowers raising their dainty fragrant heads to greet her. We can catch the perfume of the blossoms as they cast their incense in her pathway. We can hear the birds caroling and heralding her passing. All nature is alert and eager to honor its Queen as she

51

smilingly steps along the sylvan pathway and over the windswept hills, joyfully carrying the glorious King of nature in her bosom. How happy she was and how carefree and yet how contemplative! The fragrance, the melody, the color, the aliveness all about her — she realized were tributes to the God within her. "And she entered the house of Zechariah and saluted Elizabeth."

IV. Petition

May we make our lives a constant thoughtful visitation to and with Jesus and Mary.

V. Points of Meditation

1. On the second day of July [the thirty-first of May since the reform of the liturgy following Vatican II], the Church celebrates the Feast of the Visitation. As we know this feast commemorates the visit of Our Blessed Lady to her cousin Elizabeth. In the life of our Divine Lord and his Blessed Mother the outstanding events are often called mysteries, and the Church designates this visit as the Second Joyful Mystery of the Rosary, the Visitation.

Why does the Church call what seems to be just an ordinary act of courtesy a mystery? Certainly the word is not used in the very same sense, and with the same force, as it is used when applied to the Most Holy Trinity, the Incarnation, and the Redemption. But anything wonderful, anything extraordinary, anything which the eye cannot grasp in a single glance, or the mind comprehend in a split second, may in the broad sense of the word be called a mystery.

When the Queen of England visits the slums, when she goes to a poor mining district, has a cup of tea in a miner's home, kisses his wife, and caresses their baby, it is front-page news in the paper.

Her condescension has about it the element of wonder, the element of mystery.

Between Mary and Elizabeth there is a far greater gap than that which separates the Queen of England from her poverty-stricken subjects, the miners. Mary is also a Queen, the Queen of an eternal kingdom, the Queen of All Saints. All generations call her blessed. A thousand years from now who will remember what queens reigned in England during the twentieth century? A few historians and perhaps a few students of history with prodigious memories will recall them, but that is all.

Elizabeth, being a saint herself, could appreciate the gap that separated her from Mary, the Queen of All Saints. Filled with amazement at the honor Mary was paying her in journeying so far to make this visit, she gave vent to her feelings in those words which Sacred Scripture records as: "How is it that the Mother of my Lord should come to me?" Elizabeth was the expectant mother of the last and greatest of the prophets, John the Baptist. Of John, our Divine Lord would later say, "Among those born of women there has not risen one greater than John the Baptist." Mary was the expectant mother of the Son of God.

2. With haste Mary went into the hill country where Elizabeth lived, for Jesus was in haste to be about his Father's business. Though still unborn, he was anxious to begin the conquest of the empire of sin. It is as if it pained him to be in the world even for so short a time without sin feeling the weight of his unborn arm. Out of Mary there was no sin to cast. The fruits of redemption had already been applied to her soul, with the result that she had been conceived and born without Original Sin. But the child in Elizabeth's womb was bound by the chains of the sin of Adam and Eve. Inspired by her Divine Son, Mary, the Singular Vessel of Devotion, will bring her precious burden near where John is, and her unborn Child will destroy the sin and abolish the curse of the unborn Baptist. With exaltation will John leap in Elizabeth's womb, and his

now sinless soul will worship, with abounding gladness, his Redeemer and his God, hidden in the virgin womb of Mary.

Thirty-odd years later, when the Pharisees will demand to know why John baptized, if he were not the Messiah, they will receive this answer: "I baptize with water, but there shall come one mightier than I, the latchet of whose shoes I am not worthy to loose. He shall baptize with the Holy Spirit and fire." So it is no mere poetic license, no literary exaggeration, that we attach to this visit of Mary to Elizabeth the word "mystery."

Mary's life has been and still is a continual series of visitations of which that first visit to Elizabeth was the prototype. She is ever bringing Jesus to souls, and leading souls to Jesus. Alone she never comes, for Jesus is always with her. To her we owe every Holy Communion we receive, for it is the same Body, conceived and nourished in her immaculate womb, that is the food of our souls. To her we owe every spiritual visitation of Divine Grace, for she is the Mediatrix of all graces, interceding and obtaining for us favors and blessings even before we are aware of their necessity. To her we owe every good accomplished, every evil avoided, every temptation overcome, for "without him we can do nothing." If he is with us or near us, in some way she is responsible for his nearness.

3. Your daily sacrifices are your visitation to Jesus and Mary, to honor them, to offer thanksgiving, to make reparation, and to petition some new blessing. But before you began to make these sacrifices, or even to plan them, Mary has already made a visitation to you inspiring you to make them.

In the Gospel for Christmas there are two lines which, no matter how often they are read, always have a sad, melancholy tone: "He came unto his own, and his own received him not." "There was no room for them in the inn." Your coming on this pilgrimage of Our Lady is a sign that you have made room for them in the inn of your heart. They have come unto their own, and their own have received them.

VI. Thought for the Day

It has been said, "Happy is the house which the Mother of God visits." We might say, "Happy is the *heart* which the Mother of God visits." May we have the virtue of thoughtfulness as seen in the Visitation of Mary.

VII. Concluding Prayer

"Memorare."

MARY'S PRUDENCE

I. Introductory Prayer
"Presence of God."

II. Text

On this feast of St. Matthew it is very fitting that we meditate on Mary's Prudence and take as our text, "Holy Mary, Virgin Most Prudent, pray for us."

III. Setting

Cardinal Newman presents us with a picture of the Virgin Most Prudent that we might contemplate this morning, "It may not appear at first sight how the virtue of prudence is connected with the trials and sorrows of Our Lady's life; yet there is a point of view from which we are reminded of her prudence by these trials. It must be recollected that she is not only the great instance of the contemplative life but also of the practical; and the practical life is at once a life of penance and prudence if it is to be well discharged. Now Mary's life was full of eternal work and hard service. Of course her duties varied according to the seasons of her life, as a young maiden, as a wife, as a mother, as a widow; but still her life was full of duties day by day and hour by hour. As a stranger in Egypt, she had duties towards the poor heathen among whom she was thrown. As a dweller at Nazareth, she had duties towards her kinsfolk and neighbors. She had duties though unrecorded during those years in which our Lord was preaching and proclaiming His Kingdom. After he had left the earth, she had duties towards the Apostles and especially towards the Evangelists. She had duties towards the martyrs and confessors in prison — to the sick — the ignorant — the poor. Afterwards she had to seek with St. John another and a heathen country where her happy death took place. Her life was full of duties and she was full of merit. All her acts were perfect, all were the best that could be done. Now always to be awake, guarded, fervent, so as to be able to act not only without sin, but in the best possible way, in the varying circumstances of each day — denotes a life of untiring mindfulness. Of such a life prudence is the presiding virtue — so we are able to say, Virgin Most Prudent" (*Book of Meditations*).

IV. Petition

Through the intercession of Mary, Virgin Most Prudent, we ask for the virtue of Prudence.

V. Points of Meditation

1. The prudent man reflects before he acts. In doubt, he takes counsel. He is neither precipitate nor dilatory. He is prepared for obstacles and, meeting them, overcomes them. The word prudence — a contraction of providence — indicates a tendency to look ahead. It is an intellectual habit which enables a person to determine, in any given circumstance, what is virtuous and therefore desirable, and what is not; it shows the mind the correct way

to arrive at the one and avoid the other. Prudence makes no distinction in respect to theological or moral virtues in its directive activity; it presides over the production of all acts proper to each virtue, and is the universal guiding star which gives direction to all. While prudence thus aims at perfecting not the will but the intellect, and is directly concerned with determining the course of action to be taken, it does not neglect to provide the directive principle of the moral action, and is rightly called a moral virtue. Next to this virtue of prudence there is a corresponding gift of the Holy Spirit, the gift of counsel. This gift provides a person with prompt and right judgment, not by careful search of the mind, but by way of supernatural intuition. St. Thomas remarks that, in his search of guidance man has to be directed by God. It is the Spirit of counsel which makes us wise in the ways of God.

2. While Our Lady's behavior at the Annunciation bespeaks her faith and humility and her readiness to do God's will, it also gives evidence of her supreme prudence. Pondering within herself what the salutation of the angel augured, Mary kept her peace, and awaited further details from the mouth of Gabriel.

"And the angel said to her: 'Do not be afraid, Mary, for you have found favor with God. For behold, you shall conceive and bring forth a son; and you shall call his name Jesus. He shall be great, and shall be called the son of the Most High. The Lord God will give him the throne of David his father, and he shall be king over the house of Jacob forever; and of his kingdom there shall be no end'" (Lk 1:30-33).

Even this explanation left Mary uncertain as to the nature of the promised child. Was it not possible that the angel spoke of an eminently prominent, earthly king? Thus, not desiring to go against the words of Gabriel, which were evidently God's own, she inquired cautiously how this should happen, since she did not know man.

"And the angel answered and said to her: 'The Holy Spirit shall come upon you and the power of the Most High shall overshadow you; therefore the Holy One to be born shall be called the Son of God'" (Lk 1:35).

It was then that all doubts concerning her selection as the mother of the Messiah were removed, and Mary spoke her classic answer: "Behold the handmaid of the Lord; be it done to me according to your word" (Lk 1:38).

Another illustration of Our Lady's supreme prudence is recorded in St. Matthew. "When Mary had been betrothed to Joseph, she was found, before they came together, to be with child" (Mt 1:18). Rather than take it upon herself to explain to Joseph and reveal the secrets of God, she entrusted her state of perplexity to God, who sent an angel to reassure Joseph.

Instead of claiming her right of exemption, she did what every other Jewish woman was obliged to do after childbirth, and presented herself in the Temple to be purified, thus avoiding undue prominence to herself and her Child. A similar supernatural providence, perhaps with a bit of human touch, was exhibited by Mary at the marriage feast at Cana, when her discreet insistence — "Do whatever he tells you" (Jn 2:5) — brought about the first miracle of our Lord.

A final example may be drawn from Our Lady following her Son to Calvary. She was well aware that it was her Son's sacrifice; that he was to tread the winepress alone (Is 63:3). Still she felt that her presence at that fatal hour was most urgent. As the Mother of the Redeemer, her place was beneath the Cross. Who would deny that all this was done under the direct inspiration of the Holy Spirit, who wished Mary to complete her own sacrifice and share in the sacrifice of her Son.

3. These are but a few scattered examples. The Gospel is sparing with revealing details of Mary's hidden life, but to believe that she was under the continual direction of the Holy Spirit in this respect, is only an inference from her fullness of grace.

In our restless search to know the things of God and to act according to his eternal designs, we feel the urgent need of this gift of prudence. "Without it," says Father Saint Jure, "there is confusion of thought, lack of reflection, blindness in designs, hastiness in resolutions, presumption and precipitation in action." Left to our own devices, we are like those who sow a wind and reap a whirlwind. Well may we turn to Our Blessed Lady under her present title, and assure ourselves of that supernatural guidance which was hers throughout her life, and will be ours in due measure through her powerful intercession.

VI. Thought for the Day

May we use the virtue of prudence in working for heaven. May God give us the help to see clearly what is right and what is wrong and then may he give us the means to do what he wants. With the Psalmist we pray, "Show O Lord, your ways to me and teach me your paths" (Ps 24:4). Holy Mary, Virgin Most Prudent, pray for me.

VII. Concluding Prayer

"Memorare."

MARY'S FORTITUDE AND COURAGE

I. Introductory Prayer

II. Text

"A valiant woman of noble character, who can find? Her value is far beyond pearls" (Pr 31:10).

III. Setting

In Our Lady's city of Lourdes the scene on Calvary's hill has been deeply impressed in our minds. Mary knew how to endure as well as how to act with courage. Noble in her courage, she pushes her way through the crowd, climbs the hill and takes her place at the foot of the Cross. With a true spirit of fortitude, she remains for three hours erect and silent on Calvary — she accepts separation from her Son — even from his mortal remains. Then with a courageous heart, she helps to lay his body in the tomb. Is it not just then that we should proclaim her the most valiant, the most noble of women?

IV. Petition

We earnestly ask through Mary for the virtue of fortitude and the gift of fortitude. May we realize how valuable and how necessary fortitude is for the Christian who would fight the good fight of the Lord!

V. Points of Meditation

1. During the Spanish Civil War, when the Communists were trying to take over Spain, an event happened which arrested the attention of many people. The Alcazar, an ancient fortress and training school for Spanish army officers, was under the command of a Colonel Moscardo. He received an order from the so-called Loyalists to surrender the Alcazar. Knowing that they were dominated by Communists, Moscardo refused to heed their command. Immediately after his refusal, the chief of the Workers' Militia telephoned him that his young son was in their power. Unless he surrendered the Alcazar within ten minutes the boy would be shot. Upon hearing this, Colonel Moscardo challenged them to put his son on the telephone. After a brief conversation between father and son, the Chief of the Workers' Militia seized the phone from the boy and repeated his threat. Their conversation ended a moment later. In ten minutes the phone rang again, and Colonel Moscardo learned that his son had been shot.

What did Colonel Moscardo say to his young boy when he talked to him over the phone? According to the story, the son asked his father what he should do. To this question Colonel Moscardo answered, "All you can do is pray for us and die for Spain." The youngster replied to this advice, "This is quite simple; both I will do." It took extraordinary courage for the father to give such advice. No less courageous was the boy in answering and dying as he did.

Fortitude is a cardinal virtue — a moral virtue — which

enables us to overcome all difficulties in fulfilling the duties imposed on us. It is free from rashness as from fear, ready to endure as to act, to defend itself against the attacks of the enemy as to assume the offensive; it follows the straight line of the most sublime duty. It shines in all its glory when life is at stake and therefore it is the special virtue of the martyrs. The virtue of fortitude has a special beauty in man who is naturally weak. There is also a fortitude which is a "gift of the Holy Spirit which perfects the virtue of fortitude by imparting to the will an impulse and an energy enabling it to do great things joyfully and fearlessly despite all obstacles" (Tanquerey, *The Spiritual Life,* p. 621).

Colonel Moscardo and his son seemed to have the virtue and the gift of fortitude in a high degree. The Colonel had to make a difficult decision. If he surrendered, he might have saved his son. But to do so would be to betray his country, his Church and his honor as a soldier. Fortitude gave his will the energy to make the decision to sacrifice his son for Spain and for the Church.

2. Since Mary is the Queen of Martyrs as well as the Queen of All Saints, we naturally expect to find her fortitude equal to her other virtues and gifts. As we have seen, it was on Calvary's hill that she displayed this gift of the Holy Spirit in a unique degree. No doubt her relatives and friends tried to persuade her not to follow her Son to his execution on Calvary. But her own personal pain was not a motive strong enough to keep her from being near him during those last three hours. The fortitude of the Blessed Virgin Mary was clearly seen as she bore various difficulties of life in unshaken patience. She practiced fortitude in a most unusual degree on the journey to Bethlehem and the flight into Egypt. Recrimination or murmur never proceeded from her mouth. Those words which she addressed to Jesus when she found him again at Jerusalem: "Son, why have you done this to us?" were not the complaint of an impatient soul but a respectful expression of profound sorrow. "Who shall find a valiant woman" — like unto our Blessed Mother? "Her value is far beyond pearls."

3. Supernatural courage or fortitude was one of the out-

standing characteristics of Christ and his Blessed Mother. It is a mark of his followers. It overcomes our passions, especially the passion of fear, which it drives out or at least moderates. It checks the passion of anger, or directs it into channels of good. Courage helps us to carry out the duties of our state in life. All of us have difficulty in doing this. Fortitude conquers the devil who schemes and plans to lead us away from God. It assists us in working out our salvation against great obstacles, hardships and monotony. There is always some difficult angle to what we have to do, there is ever the apparent monotony of being good and doing good.

How does the virtue and gift of fortitude operate in us? Do we recoil before inconvenience, discomfort, and sacrifice? As a result of our natural dislike for pain and suffering, do we neglect duties, break commandments, and continually follow the line of least resistance? Although our lot in life may not require the heroic fortitude of Our Lady, we still need some degree of fortitude to save our souls.

Actually, the beauty of fortitude and the example of our Blessed Mother should inspire us with a holy ambition to be valiant ourselves. To be supernaturally courageous we need the help of God's grace. We may develop the virtue of fortitude by fervent continual prayer, by meditation on the passion of Christ and the dolors of Mary — and by training our wills to do what costs something — to persevere even in little things. When we overcome our natural repugnance to inconvenience, discomfort and pain and actually perform a duty just because it is a duty, the gift of fortitude is flowering by the grace of God in our lives. God is acting in us and through us but not without us.

VI. Thought for the Day

May we become more and more aware of the value of fortitude as an ornament of our souls in this age of moral weakness. Let us begin at once instead of being discouraged and giving up in our present difficulty — to lift up our hearts full of confidence in God. "My grace is sufficient for you; for power is made perfect in infirmity" (2 Cor 12:9). Our Lady, Queen of Martyrs, Queen of All Saints, pray for us.

VII. Concluding Prayer

"Memorare."

MARY, REFUGE OF SINNERS

SEPTEMBER 23RD

I. Introductory Prayer

II. Text

"Holy Mary, Mother of God, pray for us sinners now and at the hour of our death. Amen." These words of the "Hail Mary" are on our lips in a special way this morning.

III. Setting

Today in our meditation we picture Mary as the ever-ready Refuge of Sinners. She can despise no sinner, but rather, with outstretched arms, she receives all and welcomes all — the moment that they have recourse to her. St. John Damascene says that Mary is not only the refuge of the innocent but also of the wicked, who implore her protection: "I am a city of refuge to all who fly to me" (*De Dorm. B.M.*, s. 2).

O Mary, Refuge of Sinners, pray for us and save us!

V. Points of Meditation

In the Bible we read that Moses established a number of cities which were known as cities of refuge. If a man committed a crime, he might take refuge within the walls of one of these cities. There he would be safe. There he would be free from the danger of what we today call "lynch law." If he were punished, his punishment would take place only after his crime had been investigated and proved. Within the walls of one of those cities of refuge, the wrath and vengeance of the injured man dare not follow him. It would have been considered most outrageous for anyone to take the law into his own hands in a city of refuge.

When a person sins, that person is also guilty of crime — a crime against God. In the time of Moses the guilty man may have acted in a sudden passion, hastily, and with little or no reflection. Unlike the criminal in the time of Moses, the act of the sinner presupposes reflection and deliberate determination. No grave sin can ever be purely accidental. Yet the sinner, like the criminal in the days of Moses, also has a city of refuge to which he may fly. That city is none other than Our Blessed Lady herself. To be safe under the mantle of Mary the Refuge of Sinners, he has only to be sorry and to hate his sin. Then the Divine Wrath, far from pursuing him, will melt into mercy and love.

2. The questions naturally arise: How can Mary love a sinner? How can she forget what sin did to her Divine Son? The sound of the hammer, as it drove the spikes through his hands and his feet, is it not still ringing in her ears? Can his pale bloody face, as he hung on the Cross, ever be completely blotted out of her memory? How can Mary love and pity sinners who made Calvary possible?

Perhaps we can best answer these questions by a little story. The Irish poet Thomas Moore was married to one of the most beautiful women in all Ireland. Her eyes had the sparkle and luster of precious stones. Her cheeks wore the bloom of the rose. Her features were in perfect proportion. She was conscious of her beauty, and she gloried in that beauty, not through vanity, but because it was a source of joy to her husband.

Then a tragedy came into her life. She fell victim to a dreadful sickness. Smallpox struck her and brought her close to death's door. But she recovered from the dreaded scourge. When, however, she looked at her face in the mirror, she saw that it was pocked and scarred by the ravages of the disease. No longer was she the loveliest of Ireland's lovely women. Then she began to brood over her lost beauty, for she feared her husband's love for her would now grow cold. Her melancholy became so deep that friends thought she would eventually lose her mind. At last she confided the reason for her brooding to one of her friends. That friend told her secret to her poet-husband. To prove that his love for her had not died, nor even diminished, he composed that immortal poem and song:

> "Believe me, if all those endearing young charms,
> Which I gaze on so fondly today,
> Were to change by tomorrow, and flee from my arms,
> Like fairy-gifts fading away,
> Thou wouldst still be adored, as this moment thou art,
> Let thy loveliness fade as it will,
> And around the dear ruin each wish of my heart,
> Would entwine itself verdantly still."

Our souls are a million times more beautiful than the face of Thomas Moore's wife. They are made to the image and likeness of God. They reflect, in a limited degree, the eternal, infinite beauty of God. Mary realizes this fact far better than we can appreciate it. Even when our souls become pockmarked by sin, Mary still remembers their former beauty. She also knows that, unlike the lost beauty of the poet's wife, the vanished beauty of our souls can return. Real sincere sorrow for our sins, combined with a simple, straightforward confession, will do to the pockmarks of sin what no doctor and no medicine can do to the scars of smallpox.

For this reason Mary is most willing to be a refuge for those who have fallen into the mire of sin. For those who regret and bewail their sins, she is truly the Refuge of Sinners.

3. Mary hates sin, while at the same time she loves the sinner. For his crime against God she can have no affection; but for his person, his soul, she has the heart of a mother. She loves him because her maternal eye can penetrate the muck and mire of sin which cover his soul. She also realizes that God loves his soul because he has created it and made it to resemble his own image and likeness. Does not the artist love the painting over which he has labored and into which he has breathed his creative power? Does not the composer love the music in which the flame of his genius burns? So, too, does God love his masterpiece, the soul, into which he has breathed his creative power, and in which the flame of his genius burns.

Mary has three reasons for loving each soul with an intimate personal love. First, she knows that it belongs to God; it is the product of his almighty creative power. Next, it resembles to a limited extent God himself. He made it to his own image and likeness. Finally, that soul was redeemed by the Precious Blood of her Divine Son, redeemed in the Blood which she gave to him. Is there any wonder that Mary can hate sin most vehemently, and still love poor sinners? Is there any wonder now why the Church calls Mary the Refuge of Sinners?

VI. Thought for the Day

To Mary, Our Lady of Refuge, we plead with the Church: "Pray for us sinners now and at the hour of our death." Our petition is twofold: we pray for help now — that means for each moment of our life; and at the hour of our death — when we need the special grace of perseverance. Our Lady will obtain for us both graces, since she has received "the grace of maternity towards Christ's mystical body" (Marmion). Our Lady, Refuge of Sinners, pray for us.

VII. Concluding Prayer

"Memorare."

MARY'S CHEERFULNESS

I. Introductory Prayer

II. Text

"Men, you should indeed have listened to me and not have sailed from Crete, thus sparing yourselves this disaster and loss. And now I beg you to be of good cheer" (Ac 27:21-22). These words were spoken by St. Paul many centuries ago as he sailed these same waters not far from Crete. He spoke in this cheerful manner to the sailors and soldiers who were taking him as a prisoner to Rome.

III. Setting

As we recite the Litany of Loreto, we think of the Blessed Virgin Mary as Mother Most Amiable. In this beautiful title, we endeavor to describe how pleasing and loveable she is to God and men. Perhaps, one of the principal reasons for her amiability is her cheerfulness. When she embraced the mortification of Bethlehem, she did it cheerfully. What cheerfulness she manifested in exile in Egypt and in poverty at Nazareth. What unfailing strength

71

and cheerfulness she showed to us on Calvary. Never an unkind, oppressing look in Mary's eyes. Never a wounding, depressing word from Mary's lips. Never a bitter, discouraging thought in Mary's heart. Truly a Mother Most Amiable, a Mother of good cheer is Mary!

IV. Petition

We pray to Mary, Mother Most Amiable, Mother Most Cheerful for the grace of cheerfulness in our daily living.

V. Points of Meditation

We should recognize that we live in a world of defects and limitations, where no character is without a flaw and where no life is without its tempering of pain. Life with its joys and sorrows has been likened to a rose bush with its beautiful flowers and its sharp thorns. If we wish to be physically well and spiritually strong it is necessary for us to be cheerful. To be cheerful means to make little of the hardships that all of us are bound to encounter. We have to learn to look on the bright and sunnier side of things — to accentuate the pleasant and beautiful features of life and smooth over the rough spots on the road. The cheerful person in memory — as in speech — keeps dwelling on the inspiring, encouraging elements of every situation, and on the amiable characteristics of every acquaintance. We all need the power to overlook or to smile away some of the distressing details of existence. In each life much must be ignored and in each personality much must be forgiven and forgotten. It is important to have what might be called a *royal* memory. There are people who do not forget anything — the way you acted the day everything went wrong — hasty judgments that you repented as soon as they were made — words that you said before you knew it. Yes, you feel like running when you meet such people. There are others who never seem to remember anything except the good in people. They are the best loved people in the world. Only in the presence of the loving look — and the excusing word — do we consent to stand revealed in all our weakness, to humble ourselves and to enter upon the way of amendment. We all need a royal memory — if we are to possess the precious treasure of cheerfulness.

2. In trying to be cheerful, it is important to understand the personal equation in life. There is a large measure of subjectivity in our happiness and unhappiness. A man's sweetness or sourness is to be traced less often to his actual experiences than to the view that he takes of life. Happiness consists more in disposition than in position. To a certain extent pleasure and pain are necessarily relative and personal. In a great measure, a thing is distressing or not according as we do or we do not give into the inclination to so regard it... for example, a case of a mild headache. Also a man's impressions depend very much on the state in which he finds himself at the moment of a given experience — or whether he is at ease, or in a condition of excitement or nervous tension. If we are mindful of this it helps us to keep our balance and not to just go along with our feelings.

Another point to be remembered in trying to be more cheerful is that evil seems to be more conspicuous than good. In other words, it seems that what is evil and threatening attracts attention more imperatively and irresistibly than what is good. This might be nature's way of protecting us from harm. When we look into ourselves we notice that the hurts and disappointments that we experience penetrate deeper into our consciousness and memories than the strokes of good fortune and little courtesies that happen to us. The truth of the fact that evil is conspicuous is seen with regard to faultfinding and the spreading of gloom. There is an impulse in most of us to turn thoughts and conversations into channels of faultfinding. All in all, the average man is accustomed to lay far less emphasis on his pleasant than on his unpleasant experiences. That is why some people seem to take a special delight in spreading gloom. These spreaders of gloom enjoy making known facts and even suspicions of an unpleasant nature as for example "so and so dislikes you, etc."

3. If we are true followers of Jesus Christ and his Blessed Mother, we must strive after cheerfulness. St. Paul tells us that "we are saved by hope." The Church has always emphasized the fact that cheerfulness makes for godliness. St. Philip Neri and St. Francis de Sales talk about the need of being glad and cheerful. They advise us that to attain Christian perfection we must struggle against thoughts that tend to make us fearful and depressed. When we allow ourselves to become depressed, we do not do our best for God and man. The cheerful saints have always appealed to me! For them, it was a privilege and not a trial to bear thankless burdens and undertake odious responsibilities and suffer unjust reproaches, to serve the neglected and the impatient, to act as oil on the troubled waters, to be as a buffer when collisions were impending and a breakwater when the waves ran high. Those saints have showed us what a determined will with God's grace can do toward securing a happy disposition and perennial peace of mind. Although it is true that most cheerful men have been born so, many have achieved cheerfulness. With God's help, we can control our feelings of depression and their outward manifestation. We also can use our will power to control our thoughts. We can try to avoid discouraging thoughts, critical thoughts and thoughts in general that give us the blues. We can strive to count our blessings — our faith, our friends, the comfort of God's grace and his sacraments. We can think of the goodness of God and the consolation of confidence in Jesus and Mary.

VI. Thought for the Day

"And now I beg you to be of good cheer," says our fellow traveller, St. Paul. He also reminds us that we should be cheerful in the service of God, "For God loves a cheerful giver" (2 Cor 9:7).

Our pilgrimage through life should be a labor of love. O Mother, Most Amiable, grant us the gift of cheerfulness.

VII. Concluding Prayer

"Memorare."

MARY AND HOLY COMMUNION

SEPTEMBER 28TH

I. Introductory Prayer
"Presence of God."

II. Text

As we read the Last Gospel [no longer part of the Liturgy since the reforms of Vatican II] in the Holy Sacrifice of the Mass each morning we repeat the wondrous words of St. John, the Beloved Apostle, describing the mystery of the Incarnation. "And the Word was made flesh and dwelt among us" (Jn 1:14).

III. Setting

A most precious legacy was bequeathed to St. John from the Cross. Jesus, with his dying lips, made for his Mother what provision was possible. "From that hour the disciple took her to his own." St. John was careful that the memory of this sacred and exalted charge entrusted to him should never perish, so he and he alone of the evangelists, has enshrined this incident in his narrative. After the Ascension, Mary lived for years with St. John who was a priest and an apostle. As such he celebrated Holy Mass and gave her Holy Communion. Mary was thus enabled to live in the Eucharistic Presence of her Son during those years of separation. What a model she is for our devotion to Mass and Communion! In every Holy Mass we receive Christ from the hands of the priest, just as Mary was privileged to receive her Eucharistic Son from the hands of St. John.

IV. Petition

Through Our Lady of the Blessed Sacrament may my desire for Holy Communion grow day by day and may I have the grace to make a good preparation for and thanksgiving after Holy Communion.

V. Points of Meditation

1. What Jesus did for us he did for Mary in a more eminent and excellent way. This is natural and reasonable. It is what we might have expected if we had known only one fact about Mary; namely, that she was the Mother of Jesus, the Mother of God.

To us, he has been generous; to her he was magnanimous. He redeemed us. But Redemption comes to us only after we have been conceived and born with Original Sin. In her conception and before she was born, the fruits of Redemption were already applied to her soul. As a result, she was conceived and born without Original Sin. For us our Divine Lord lived three public years, during which he preached his Gospel, trained the Apostles and, before dying on the Cross, founded his Church. For Mary and with Mary, he lived thirty years of his life, unknown to the world, known only to her. The bodies of some of his saints he preserved from the corruption which takes place after death. Mary he not only preserved from the corruption of the grave, but he assumed her, body and soul, into heaven. Some of the saints lived long years sustained by no other food than the Blessed Sacrament. In the opinion of not a few writers, the Sacred Species, the Host, remained in Mary uncorrupted from one Communion to another. "For her sake," says Father Faber, "he instituted the Blessed Sacrament, principally for her, and more for her than all the people in the world put together."

2. Our Divine Lord and his Blessed Mother were like two magnets, one big and powerful, the other small and, by comparison, less powerful. These two magnets attracted each other. Jesus was her life, her sweetness, and her hope. She among the billions of his intelligent creatures was his one perfect creature, "our tainted nature's solitary boast." If St. Paul could say, and he did say, "for me to live is Christ, and to die is gain," how can we describe the longing, the aspirations of Mary for the face-to-face vision of her Son after his Ascension into heaven? The souls in Purgatory are on fire with the desire to see God. The greater part of their suffering comes from their insatiable hunger and their unquenchable thirst after the vision of God. Perhaps only a soul in Purgatory could appreciate this longing of Mary for the vision and possession of God and give us an adequate description of it. Now it was this longing on the part of Mary for union with God which made her Holy Communions so pleasing to him.

We know that a stone dropped from an airplane will fall to earth with an ever-increasing velocity. The earth attracts the stone like a magnet. That attraction becomes stronger and stronger as the stone approaches the earth. That is why the speed of a falling stone increases with each second that it falls.

There is also a natural attraction which God exerts on every human soul. As the seconds of our life tick away, we should be moving closer to God. We should feel that attraction of God on our souls growing stronger. The saints felt it. Mary felt it in a supereminent degree. The closer a person is to God, the greater will be the attraction, and the more sensitive should the soul be to it.

3. Why do some of us feel that attraction so faintly as to seem

not to feel it at all? The answer could be the manner in which we receive Holy Communion. There is enough spiritual energy, there is enough grace in one Holy Communion to make us saints. In the opinion of St. Alphonsus Liguori a single Holy Communion is sufficient to make a saint. When we are not saints after we have received the Blessed Sacrament, the fault lies with us, not with the Sacrament.

The spiritual energy, the grace which comes with each reception of Holy Communion, we absorb only in proportion to our dispositions at the time we receive. Again, some proportion exists between our preparation and thanksgiving for Holy Communion and the grace we receive from the Blessed Sacrament. A hunger and thirst for union with our Divine Lord will result in a good preparation and thanksgiving. Sometimes we start our preparation for Holy Communion with no very great longing for union with our Lord, but our preparation results in an increased desire for him. Here preparation becomes the cause of our longing for union with our Divine Savior. Ordinarily it is the effect of an intense desire to be united with him and to be less unworthy of this union by reason of our preparation. From experience we learn that little or no desire for Holy Communion will result in no preparation or only a minimum of preparation. In return, we should not be surprised to receive from the Blessed Sacrament only a minimum of divine grace.

In this matter, as in all other matters, God has given us free will. He will not force us to prepare to receive him. He will not force us to thank him for his unspeakable gift after we have received. Even God's grace does not take away our free will, nor does it perform miracles. The grace of God operates when, and only when, we cooperate with it.

Well does St. Francis de Sales describe the relationship of grace and free will and their mutual cooperation in our good works:

"Grace is so gracious, and so graciously seizes our hearts to draw them, that it in no way offends the liberty of our will. It touches powerfully, yet so delicately the springs of our spirit that our free will suffers no violence from it. Grace has power, not to force but to entice the heart. It has a holy violence not to violate our liberty but to make it full of love. It acts strongly, yet so sweetly, that our will is not overwhelmed by so powerful an action. It presses us but does not oppress our liberty, so that under the very action of its power, we consent to or resist its movements as we wish."

Let us beg of God the grace to hunger and thirst for Holy Communion. Through Mary's intercession, let us ask for the spiritual help to make better preparations and thanksgivings. On our part, let us determine to cooperate with the operations of grace constantly taking place in our soul.

VI. Thought for the Day

With Our Lady of the Blessed Sacrament, the Mediatrix of all Graces, we will prepare well for the coming of the Lord each morning at Mass. "And the Word was made flesh and dwelt among us" (Jn 1:14). The same Jesus who was always with her is the same Jesus who is always with us — Body and Blood, soul and divinity — in the Eucharist. With the help of Our Lady of the Blessed Sacrament, we will live the life of Christ in the Holy Sacrifice of the Mass and in our daily lives. "And I live now not I; but Christ lives within me" (Gal 2:20).

VII. Concluding Prayer

"Memorare."

THE SYMPATHY OF
JESUS AND MARY

OCTOBER 6TH

I. Introductory Prayer

II. Text

"As the sufferings of Christ abound in us so also by Christ does our comfort abound." Those are the words of St. Paul as found in his Second Letter to the Corinthians the first chapter, the fifth verse.

III. Setting

In the town of Bethany a certain man named Lazarus died. He was the brother of Mary and Martha. "Now Jesus loved Martha, and her sister Mary, and Lazarus" (Jn 11:5). The intensity of his sympathy may be partly estimated from the fact that Jesus endangered his life by going to see Lazarus. His disciples, quite disturbed about his intended visit to Bethany, said to him, "Rabbi, the Jews only recently sought to stone you and you're going back there again?" (Jn 11:8). The loving sympathy of Jesus knew no fear. When Jesus drew near the home of Lazarus, Martha greeted him with a simple profession of faith, "Lord, if you had been here, my brother would not have died. Still, I know that whatever you ask of God, God will give it to you." Without a moment's hesitation, the sympathetic heart of Jesus gave the consoling answer — the promise of a miracle. "Your brother shall rise again." Jesus of Nazareth did not delay. He went right to the source of the sorrow and applied an unfailing remedy. Martha said to him, "I know that he shall rise again in the resurrection at the last day." Then the Sacred Heart spoke a few words of sympathy to Martha. These words have carried and will continue to carry in the centuries to come consolation to millions of saddened hearts. "I am the Resurrection and the Life. He who believes in me, although he be dead shall live. And every one who lives and believes in me, shall not die forever. Do you believe this?" Martha's ready answer was another manifestation of her living faith. "Yes, Lord, I do believe that you are the Christ, the Son of the living God, who have come into this world."

When Martha's sister, Mary, came to Jesus, "She fell down at his feet and said, 'Lord, if you had been here, my brother would not have died." The Sacred Heart of Jesus was deeply moved. "Where have you laid him?" he asked. They said, "Lord, come and see." The tears of Mary, the sight of the tomb of Lazarus, the simple childlike faith of the sorrowing sisters and their perfect resignation to God's will — all this was too much for the sympathetic heart of Jesus. St. John tells us, "And Jesus wept." We all know the rest of the narrative — how Jesus restored Lazarus to life, and we can easily imagine the happiness that followed. This is a beautiful revelation of the Sacred Heart's sympathetic love. All of us can become the object of the same loving sympathy of the Savior — if we only seek it with the living faith of Martha and Mary. "As the sufferings of Christ abound in us, so also by Christ does our comfort abound" (2 Cor 1:5).

IV. Petition

Our petition this morning is that our hearts may be sympathetic hearts fashioned after the Sacred Heart of Jesus and the Immaculate Heart of Mary.

V. Points of Meditation

1. Sympathy has been described as winged charity. Sympathy is the nurse for the illness of the soul. It is the feeling of compassion for another's suffering. Sympathy anticipates the slow mind. It is prophetic. It foresees. Sympathy is spontaneous. It is the promptness of charity. Just as charity is of the heart, so sympathy is nothing more than winged charity. The passage of Isaiah describing a lack of sympathy helps us to understand the true nature of sympathy. It is quoted by St. Matthew, "And the prophecy of Isaiah is fulfilled in them, who says, 'By hearing you shall hear, and not understand, and seeing you shall see and shall not perceive. For the heart of this people is grown gross'" (Mt 13:14). The heart that is gross is dull in feeling. Such a heart is not sympathetic. Instead of being sensitive, the gross heart is callous; instead of being prophetic, it is blind. Such a heart is not winged charity. It is tied to itself and caged within the narrow limits of selfishness. There are three requisites for a truly sympathetic heart: l) unselfishness; 2) knowledge; 3) experience. Sympathy is essentially unselfish. It does not walk with pride. It is the charitable heart looking outward. Besides unselfishness, sympathy calls for knowledge. We must know another's sorrow and pain to feel for him. The richest sympathy is produced by knowledge, vivified by experience. No one is so well able to give sympathy as one who has known the want of it; as one who wishes to save others from drinking the cup which he himself has deeply drunk.

2. These three requisites for a truly sympathetic heart, namely unselfishness, knowledge and experience are fully veri-

fied in the Sacred Heart of Jesus and the Immaculate Heart of Mary. Since the Heart of Jesus was God's gift to us, it was utterly unselfish. It was made for others: "God so loved the world that he sent his only begotten Son." As for knowledge and experience, "Christ read the hearts of men." "He knew their thoughts; he knew what was in man." Just as Christ was the searcher of hearts, he was also the man of sorrows. The prophecy of Isaiah described the pain and sorrow that he experienced, "Despised, and the most abject of men, a man of sorrows, and acquainted with infirmity; and his look was as it were hidden and despised, whereupon we esteemed him not. Surely he has born our infirmities and carried our sorrow; and we have thought of him as it were a leper and as one struck by God and afflicted. But he was wounded for our iniquities, he was bruised for our sins; the chastisement of our peace was upon him and by his bruises we were healed" (Is 53). Unselfishness, knowledge and experience — the Sacred Heart possessed these qualities to an eminent degree. The Heart of Jesus was sympathy itself. The life story of Jesus as found in the Gospels is a story of a heart of sympathy. "And seeing the multitude, he had compassion on them because they were distressed, and lying like sheep that have no shepherd" (Mt 9:36). How wonderfully he showed his sympathy towards discouraged sinners, towards the sorrow-stricken widow of Naim, towards the children who flocked around him. His treatment of Magdalen, of the adulteress and of the good thief, the parable of the lost sheep, the divine parable of the prodigal son, these are the imperishable moments of his sympathy. "As the sufferings of Christ abound in us, so also by Christ does our comfort abound" (2 Cor 1:5).

Sympathy was also an outstanding virtue of our Blessed Mother. Mary's sympathy was enjoyed by St. Joseph amid the hardship of searching for a lodging at Bethlehem and during the difficult journey to the foreign country of Egypt. Her sympathetic heart went out to the young married couple and their relatives at the marriage feast of Cana. Her heart was filled with sympathy for her beloved Crucified Son as she stood on Calvary's hill. In the days that followed all the Apostles experienced the loving sympathy of Mary, the Queen of the Apostles. We, too, have witnessed and continue to witness the motherly sympathy of Mary for all people at Lourdes and at Fatima... and wherever people show themselves to be her sons and daughters as she has showed herself to be their Mother.

3. Our hearts should be modeled after the Sacred Heart of Jesus and the Immaculate Heart of Mary. Since their hearts were filled with sympathy for fallen humanity, this virtue should play an important part in the life of each one of us. Sympathy has wonderful power in changing great sinners into most devoted and self-sacrificing saints. We are too often like the cold repellent Pharisees and too little inclined to help those who have fallen. Our Lady and Our Master's example should stimulate and help us to be tenderly sympathetic towards our discouraged and disappointed fellowman. Then they, too, like the disciples on the road to Emmaus may feel their hearts burning within them with a quickening appreciation not only of the human consolation we may give them but also of the higher divine consolation that our words and acts of sympathy help them better to understand and seek in all their sorrows. In our own spiritual life, sympathy is a great aid to us in our struggle for sanctity. Sympathy conquers pride, the arch-enemy of the spiritual life. The sympathetic heart is filled with a living knowledge of Christ crucified. Our sympathy for Jesus is an accurate indicator of our love for Jesus. Only a saint can put himself completely in the place of Christ, can suffer with him and be truly and perfectly sympathetic.

VI. Thought for the Day

On the evening before Jesus Christ died, he gave us the Holy Eucharist — the sacrament of sympathy. At that last supper the sympathetic Heart of Jesus clearly revealed itself when he said, "Let not your heart be troubled. You believe in God, believe also in me" (Jn 14:5). "And I will ask the Father and he shall give you another Paraclete that he may abide with you forever" (Jn 14:16). "Peace I leave with you, my peace I give to you. Not as the world gives do I give to you. Let not your heart be troubled, nor let it be afraid" (Jn 14:27). "I am the vine; you the branches; he who abides in me, and I in him, will bear much fruit, for without me you can do nothing" (Jn 15:5). "As the Father has loved me, I also have loved you. Abide in my love" (Jn 15:9).

VII. Concluding Prayer

"Memorare."

MARY'S ROSARY

Feast of the Holy Rosary

I. Introductory Prayer

II. Text

"Mary, Queen of the Most Holy Rosary, pray for us." These are the words that we pray frequently in the Litany of Loreto.

III. Setting

Whenever we shall pray the Rosary or speak about it in the future, we shall undoubtedly recall the city of the Rosary — Lourdes, and "the beautiful lady dressed in white, girdled with a blue sash," who joined with Bernadette in the perfect prayer. We shall recall our visit to the place where Our Lady of Fatima spoke to Lucy, Francisco and Jacinta saying, "Say the Rosary everyday — to bring peace to the world." Certainly, we shall never forget the happy days of this pilgrimage which have been linked together by the recitation of Mary's Rosary. On this feast day of Our Lady, we join with her children throughout the world in honoring her as the

Queen of the Most Holy Rosary. May our devotion to our Blessed
Mother increase each day as we walk accompanied by our rosary
through life.

IV. Petition

Our petition is taken from the collect prayer of this morning's
Holy Mass. "Grant we beseech you, O Lord, that meditating on
these mysteries of the Most Holy Rosary of the Blessed Virgin
Mary, we may imitate what they contain, and obtain what they
promise."

V. Points of Meditation

1. For centuries the Rosary has been the privileged prayer of
Catholics. Although it is addressed to the Blessed Lady, it is
chiefly a prayer of praise and thanksgiving to the Son. Adapted to
every state of mind, it offers to God a song of perpetual homage for
the divine mercy shown to his Mother. When Mary prayed her
"Magnificat" and said, "Henceforth all generations shall call me
blessed" (Lk 1:48), she could have hardly anticipated to what
extent that prophecy would be fulfilled. Ever since the veneration
of the Mother of God began to take shape in apostolic times, the
faithful have repeated the angelical salutation as a reminder of
Mary's glorious participation in the work of the redemption. The
gathering of these prayers into a garland of roses, which we call
the Rosary, is only an expression of the untiring efforts of her
children to perpetuate devotion to Our Blessed Lady. Father
Lacordaire says: "Love has but few words to utter; and while it is
ever repeating these words, it never repeats itself."

2. Without going into the disputed question of the origin of
the Rosary, we may say that the use of prayer beads to count
identical prayers dates back to time immemorial. In the Christian

world the use of "paternosters" is centuries old. As the word clearly indicates, these appliances were originally used to count "Our Fathers." In the twelfth century the "Hail Mary" as a formula of prayer came into use and, in the course of that century, the custom of reciting 50 or 150 "Ave Marias" became a common practice. No doubt the same method was employed to count the "Hail Marys" and the common rosary beads, as we know them today, are still designated by the name "paternosters" in several European countries.

In the thirteenth century St. Dominic was given the Rosary by Our Lady. Armed with it, he found success in bringing back to the faith a great many Albigensians, an heretical group in southern France. In addition, the Christian army warring against the Albigensians were instructed by St. Dominic to recite the Rosary before the battle of Muret (1213). Their leader, De Montfort ascribed the victory that followed to the prayers of the Rosary. He built the first chapel of the Rosary at Muret in thanksgiving for their success.

The fifteenth century gave a great impetus to the general practice of reciting the Rosary by the establishment of Rosary Confraternities under Dominican auspices. An acceptance of a more uniform system in its recitation is without doubt to be ascribed to the tireless effort of the Dominican Fathers, for which reason the Rosary in the Western Church is properly called the Dominican Rosary. In 1571 a special feast in honor of Our Lady of Victory was instituted by Pope St. Pius V for the first Sunday of October, in commemoration and gratitude for the naval victory of Lepanto gained by Don Juan of Austria over the Turkish Fleet. This victory was due to the protection of Our Blessed Lady and it corresponded wonderfully with the processions made at Rome on that same day by the members of the Rosary Confraternity. Two years later, upon request of the Dominican Order, Gregory XIII changed the name of this feast to that of the Holy Rosary, and permitted the commemoration to be kept in all churches which possessed an altar dedicated to the Holy Rosary. The observance was extended by Clement X in 1671, to the whole of Spain, and in 1716, upon another important victory gained over the Turks in Hungary, Clement XI ordered the feast to be observed by the universal Church. Benedict XIII first gave the feast a set of proper lessons in the second nocturne, while Leo XIII raised the observance to the rank of a double of the second class, and added the present invocation to the Litany of Loreto (1883).

The celebration of the feast is now kept on the date of the Battle of Lepanto, October 7th, except by the Dominicans who still observe the original first Sunday of October. Throughout her eighteen appearances at Lourdes Our Lady carried the Rosary. In the course of her appearances at Fatima in 1917, Our Blessed Mother said, "I am the Lady of the Rosary. I have come to ask the faithful to amend their lives and ask pardon for their sins. They must not continue to offend our Lord. They must say the Rosary."

3. In the Rosary we have a wonderful blessing of Mother and Son. It is the Gospel transformed into prayer. It is the life of Jesus as seen through the eyes of Mary. St. Charles Borromeo rightly called the Rosary the most divine of all devotions. It is everyone's prayer. Pope Pius XI (1937), in writing his encyclical on peace through the Rosary called it the Virgin's Psalter — the breviary of the Gospel and the Christian life — the source of strength for the apostolate. The Rosary is truly life's companion and it considers the three great mysteries of salvation: the incarnation, the redemption, and the life beyond the grave. It places before us, in concrete form, the life of our Lord, who came down from the Father and who returned to him after his life's work was completed. It contains the whole of Christian dogma in all its splendor and elevation, like a true book of morality and spirituality which is presented to us in the combined example of Jesus and Mary. It is a very practical form of prayer since the mysteries of the Rosary are designed to be reproduced in the life of every Christian. For in our progress toward God there are likewise three stages. The first one, that of knowledge, is represented by the joyful mysteries, which contain the goodness of the incarnation and open to us the

way of salvation. The second stage is the one of effort and labor. It indicates our way, which is often painful to nature, but which is ever shaped after our Lord's own example. The final stage is that of rest in the possession of eternal life. The Rosary is a true introduction to even the highest forms of prayer, one of intimate converse with Jesus and Mary. It has been called a school of contemplation and for many saints such as St. Dominic, St. Ignatius, St. Francis Xavier, St. Francis de Sales, St. Vincent de Paul, it has been just that. To them it is more than a devotion, more than a formula of prayer; it is a form of life, one which leads them through the several stages of purification to the most desirable union with God.

VI. Thought for the Day

As we pray the Rosary with renewed fervor may we learn the lesson of joy in the Joyful Mysteries — the lesson of sorrow in the Sorrowful Mysteries — and the lesson of glory in the Glorious Mysteries. Pope Benedict XV expressed the sentiments of all the Popes when he said, "This prayer is perfect because of the praise it offers, because of the lessons it imparts, because of the graces it obtains and because of the triumph it achieves." Mary, Queen of the Most Holy Rosary, pray for us.

VII. Concluding Prayer

"Memorare."

MARY'S WISDOM

SEPTEMBER 30TH
St. Jerome

I. Introductory Prayer

II. Text

In the litany of Our Lady of Loreto we find many beautiful titles and the one on which we might meditate this morning is "Seat of Wisdom, pray for us."

III. Setting

The scene of our meditation is with Jesus and Mary. We think of how the Son of God, who is called in Scripture the Word and Wisdom of God, once dwelt in Mary and then after she brought him forth into the world, he was carried in her arms and seated on her lap in his first years. Thus she became the human throne of him who reigns in heaven — and we proclaim her "Seat of Wisdom." The possession of her Son lasted beyond his infancy. He was under her gentle rule, as St. Luke tells us, and lived with her until he went forth to preach in his public life, that is, for at least 30 years. During those many years, she must have gained great wisdom from his conversations of present, past and future. Although she was a poor woman without human advantages, she must in her knowledge of creation, of the universe and of history, have excelled the greatest of philosophers, and in her theoretical knowledge the greatest of theologians, and in her prophetic discernment, the most favored of prophets. What was the grand theme of conversation between Mother and Son but the nature, the attributes, the providence and the works of almighty God. Would not our Lord be ever glorifying the Father who sent him? Would he not unfold to her the solemn eternal decrees, and the purposes and will of God? God spoke to the prophets but he spoke to them in figure and parable. To Moses alone, he spoke face to face. Moses had the privilege now and then. Mary for 30 years sat and heard Him — spoke to him face to face — asked him questions, and the answers that she received were from the eternal God — who neither deceives nor can be deceived. Rightly is the Blessed Virgin Mary called "Seat of Wisdom."

IV. Petition

We pray that we may have a profound reverence for the gift of wisdom and we earnestly desire to possess it always.

V. Points of Meditation

Wisdom is the most precious gift of the Holy Spirit, for it is properly the fruit of charity, the most excellent treasure that one may ever possess in this life. It consists in a disposition of our mind to regard and regulate all things by the light of the divine law. The gift of wisdom seems to partake of the qualities of all the other gifts. Wisdom is pious; wisdom is prudent. It is fearful, for fear of the Lord is its very beginning. Wisdom is courageous in the face of danger, and capable of enduring, like the gift of fortitude. Similar to the gift of knowledge, wisdom also knows, for its relish of divine things is closely connected to its sense of values for created things. Like understanding, it possesses a keen appreciation for the mysteries of religion, and its delight is to penetrate deeper and deeper into them. Wisdom has been defined as "a gift which perfects the virtue of charity by enabling us to discern God and divine things in their ultimate principles and by giving us a relish for them" (Tanquerey, *The Spiritual Life*, p. 629).

In the Book of Psalms, the holy writer tells us to "taste and see that the Lord is sweet" (Ps 33:9). By the gift of wisdom we see, for it is a light to the mind. It is an eye to our soul, a telescopic eye, for it sees all the way back to God. Through Wisdom we see God as the cause of all things and at the same time the end or purpose for which all things were created. But wisdom does more than just see. It enables us to experience, to taste and relish, things divine. By this gift we appreciate the meaning of our Lord's words, "My yoke is easy and my burden light." The highest of the gifts of the Holy Spirit perfects the highest of the virtues. Wisdom perfects charity. At the same time it deepens our faith and strengthens our hope.

2. By the gift of Wisdom, Mary saw the divine plan of creation and redemption as a vast mosaic. The beauty of this mosaic reflected the supreme beauty of God himself. Its vastness was a shadow of his infinity. The countless number of stones in the mosaic, all perfectly fitted together and blending into a wealth of color, mirrored his boundless power and his infallible wisdom. She saw her own Divine Son with the Body born of her flesh and blood as the central figure of this mosaic. Clustered round about him she saw her own self with St. Joseph, John the Baptist, all the Apostles, as well as myriad other saints who would glorify him in a greater or lesser degree. She saw the Cross by which he would draw all things to himself, a dark shadow to those rejecting it, a blaze of glory for those embracing it. All this and much more, the

94

gift of wisdom enabled her to see. She saw, she marveled, she relished. Joy, love and happiness flooded her soul.

The title "Seat of Wisdom" is full of meaning. Of course, this title finds its origin and foundation in the grace of her divine maternity. By this grace Mary has become the bodily dwelling place of the uncreated Wisdom. She became the Bride of the Holy Spirit. Mary is also called the Seat of Wisdom because of the special office which she holds in the internal organization of the Church, where she communicates the graces merited by her Son. "In me is all grace of the way and the truth, in me is all hope of life, and of virtue. Come to me, all you who desire me, and be filled with my fruits" (Si 24:25-26). Mary is regarded as the figure of wisdom in her continual, universal, and personal activity and power, which make it necessary for men to seek grace from her and in relation to her.

3. What should be our attitude with regard to the gift of wisdom? To say the very least, we should esteem it highly. If the gift of wisdom is to mold and shape our life, it will do so only because we have longed for it ardently, prayed for it incessantly, and pursued it relentlessly.

It will not grow alone — like a wild flower. Its presence and growth presuppose a similar development of all the other gifts. Without the constant practice of the moral virtues, humility, meekness, purity and obedience, it will remain dwarfed and stunted. We must try to see all things proceeding from God as their author, reflecting his various attributes, and returning to him as their last end. This work is hard and the process is long, but the reward is satisfying. It is "to taste and see that the Lord is sweet" (Ps 33:9).

VI. Thought for the Day

As we offer the Holy Sacrifice of the Mass on this feast of St. Jerome, we ask him as a faithful follower of wisdom to intercede for us with God, our Father, that we too may have this priceless gift. "In the midst of the Church the Lord opened his mouth and filled him with the spirit of wisdom and understanding." These are the words of the Introit of his Mass today. The grace that we ask is that we may have a relish for right things. "*Da nobis in eodem Spiritu recta sapere.*" May we endeavor to look upon men, things and events as God views them in a spirit of true wisdom.

VII. Concluding Prayer

"Memorare."

MARY'S FEAR OF THE LORD

SUNDAY, OCTOBER 5TH

I. Introductory Prayer

II. Text

The words of our text this morning are taken from the Book of Isaiah 11:2-3, "And the spirit of the Lord shall rest upon him... and he shall be filled with the spirit of fear of the Lord."

III. Setting

As we already know a great modern miracle took place on October 13, 1917. As 70,000 persons watched apprehensively, the sun, whirling like a gigantic fire-wheel, plunged at dizzying speed toward the earth. It was the culmination of a series of mysterious events which had occurred in the obscure Portuguese village of Fatima, events which were to have earthshaking consequences. For the Blessed Virgin Mary, Mother of God, had appeared on earth in person to three humble children and in a series of apparitions, had predicted World War II, the rise of Communism, the present world chaos. But even more important than her prophecies were the promises that she made — that if her wishes

97

were followed, Russia would be converted and mankind would know peace. Our Lady of Fatima, in her plan of penance and prayer, has taught us filial fear of the Lord urging all of us to reverence and respect God, Our Father.

IV. Petition

O Lord, Jesus, through the intercession of your Blessed Mother, give me an ample share of this salutary fear in accordance with what you said through the prophet, Jeremiah 32:40, "I will place my fear in their hearts."

V. Points of Meditation

1. Many people consider all fear as an unmixed evil. Franklin D. Roosevelt once said, "The only thing we have to fear is fear itself." This statement appealed to a great many people. It made a deep impression on those who regard all fear as unmixed evil. Yet some fear, even when it is not the kind of fear which is a gift of the Holy Spirit, can be a good and useful quality. A boy fears that he will fail an examination in school. As a result he studies more diligently and is successful due to this added effort. Because of his fear that his house may burn down, a person protects his property with adequate fire insurance. Many drivers avoid an auto accident because their fear of harming themselves and others makes them drive more cautiously. Of course, unreasonable fears are evil and they can be very harmful to human progress and happiness. Fear which is obsessive, fear which paralyzes our thinking and acting, is certainly bad.

The Holy Ghost teaches us that "the fear of the Lord is the beginning of wisdom" (Ps 111:10). This fear is not that servile movement which has for its object the chastisement due to sin; it is a sentiment of filial piety, grounded on the one hand on the greatness and majesty of God, and on the other of the deformity

98

of sin. Servile fear may be found even among those who do not love God whom the dread of punishment alone keeps back from offending their Lord and Master. On the other hand, filial fear belongs to God's children. These recognize the Most High for their Sovereign Lord, and love him as their tender Father. They have profound esteem and veneration for him. Knowing that they are exposed in this life to a thousand occasions of offending him, by reason of the temptations they must undergo through the frailty of the flesh, the malice of the devil, and the allurements of the world, they fear sin above every other evil. Fear of the Lord may be defined as "the Gift of the Holy Spirit which inclines our will to a filial respect for God, removes us from sin, displeasing to him, and gives us hope in the power of his help" (Tanquerey, *The Spiritual Life*, p. 623). This gift of fear of the Lord makes us vividly conscious of the greatness of God, extremely sensitive to the least fault offensive to him and habitually watchful and vigilant in cooperating with grace to avoid sin and to do God's will.

2. In the Blessed Virgin Mary this gift functioned smoothly and efficiently. She is vividly conscious of the greatness of God. "My soul magnifies the Lord... because he who is mighty has done great things for me" (Lk 1:46). At the moment of the Immaculate Conception, Mary received, together with the other gifts of the Holy Spirit, that of fear of the Lord. This was a filial and reverential fear in Mary — caused by a keen and lively sense of the awful majesty of the Most High and his limitless power. When the Blessed Mother had lost the Boy Jesus, through no fault of her own, she returned with Joseph to Jerusalem without a moment's delay. We know from the Gospel story that they searched with anxious hearts. When they found Jesus in the temple, Mary revealed her filial fear of the Lord, "Son, why have you done this to us? Your father and I have been looking for you with great anxiety" (Lk 2:48). This filial fear impelled the glorious Virgin to believe with all her heart the truths revealed by God; to consecrate to the Lord all the affections of her soul; to shelter herself and rest like a white dove under the fatherly wings of Divine Providence: "I delight to rest in his shadow" (Sg 2:3).

3. When we are baptized we receive the infused gifts of the Holy Spirit. As long as we remain in a state of sanctifying grace we continue to possess these gifts. Fear of the Lord is in us, dormant or operative. When it is operative, it is so because we have been constantly cooperating with the actual graces God sends us. This cooperation results in a development first of the infused moral virtues and eventually of the infused gifts of the Holy Spirit. Fear of the Lord is the disposition our soul requires if it is to be alert to sin and to the occasions of sin. With this disposition we have practical appreciation of the greatness and goodness of God. Not because of his power, but because of his goodness we fear to offend him. Prayer and devotion to the Holy Spirit will bring about the growth of fear of the Lord. Thus, we shall be preserved from becoming like the hardhearted people in this morning's Gospel who were invited to the marriage feast by their king. Meditation on the Goodness of God, his sanctity and his other attributes will help to keep the gift of fear of the Lord operative in our souls. Reflection on sin and its occasions can be the soil in which this gift grows, expands and develops.

VI. Thought for the Day

"Fear God and keep his commandments" (Ec 12:13). The beneficial effect of this filial fear is felt especially at the moment of death. Strengthened by this gift we will not dread the passage from life to eternity but on the contrary, we shall look upon that moment as the beginning of all real blessings. "He who fears the Lord will have a happy end; even on the day of his death he will be blessed" (Si 1:13).

VII. Concluding Prayer:

"Memorare."

MARY, QUEEN OF THE APOSTLES

OCTOBER 8TH

I. Introductory Prayer

"Presence of God."

II. Text

This morning we again turn to the Litany of Loreto for our text: "Queen of the Apostles, pray for us."

III. Setting

On our journey home our minds and hearts must frequently return to Rome, the Eternal City. This beautiful city set on the Vatican Hill will always be an inspiration to us. Our faith, our hope, our charity have been revitalized by our contact with this city which for many, many centuries has remained essentially the same — in the past as at present, at present as in the future. Our visit to the Shrine of the Prince of Apostles and to his two hundred and sixty-second successor, Pope Pius XII, has quickened within

101

us the realization that we too, must join with greater effort in the apostolic work of bringing Jesus Christ to all with whom we come in contact. We can only do this in the way that our Holy Father does it — through Mary, Queen of the Apostles. Throughout his glorious reign, he has depended on Mary to come to his aid. As the Good Shepherd he has gathered his flock together through the Marian Year, the proclamation of the dogma of the Assumption, the Immaculate Heart of Mary and the Queenship of Mary. Since to a certain extent we can measure our progress in perfection by the intensity of our devotion to Mary, we thank God for the saint that he has given us as his Vicar on earth.

IV. Petition

May we join with Pope Pius XII in being true apostles at prayer, at work and in our daily living. We can accomplish this through Mary, Queen of the Apostles.

V. Points of Meditation

1. Between a queen and her subjects there is usually some common bond, something which unites them, something which creates a natural relationship. Among earthly queens that common bond may be the land itself, the language, and the love for their native country which we call patriotism. She may be born in that land, speak its language, and love all the things which pertain to the welfare of her subjects.

We call Mary Queen of Apostles. It seems natural to ask ourselves what was the common bond uniting Mary to the Apostles. It goes without saying that Our Blessed Mother loved Jesus. She loved him intensely. She loved him with a personal love. All this is also true of the Apostles. They had the same kind of love for Jesus as Mary had. They loved him intensely, not in the same degree as

Mary, but nevertheless in a very high degree. They loved him intimately and personally. By comparison with Mary, they could never be as close to him, as intimate and personal toward him, as she was. Yet he had called them "friends," and that name, coming from his lips, meant more to them than words can describe. Mary, the Queen, and the Apostles, her subjects, had as a common bond uniting them their love for Jesus.

Closely allied to this bond of love, and springing from it, was the common desire they had to make our Divine Lord known and loved. While on earth he had said, "Now this is eternal life, that they may know you, the only true God, and Jesus Christ whom you have sent." After his Ascension into heaven Mary had but one all-embracing ambition. To make Jesus known, loved, and imitated was the consuming desire of her last years on earth. The ambition of the Apostles, like their love, differed from that of Mary only in degree. To go and teach all nations whatever he had commanded them was the driving force behind all their thinking, planning, and hoping.

It seemed but natural then that they should regard Mary as their Queen. To her they went for advice, for consolation, and for encouragement. Under these circumstances it was most fitting that the Church should confer on Mary the title "Queen of Apostles." After all, an apostle is one who has a special vocation and a definite spiritual work to accomplish. He is one who labors long and hard to bring about its accomplishment. That work consists in leading others closer to Christ.

2. In the broad sense of the word every adult Catholic is, or should be, an apostle. Few of us will go to heaven alone. Few of us will go to hell alone. Consciously or unconsciously, while saving our own souls, we shall be instrumental in helping others to save theirs. If we should lose our own souls, we shall most probably be instrumental in causing other persons to lose theirs. In this matter there is no room for neutrality. We work with our Lord or we work against him. "He who is not with me is against me; and he who gathers not with me, scatters."

Example is contagious. Good example affects others. Every act of virtue, every duty fulfilled, every principle carried out into practice has its effect on those with whom we live. We may not be conscious of this. In keeping a commandment or in practicing a virtue, our only intention may be to please God. Certainly it should be our principal intention. The possibility of influencing our neighbor may never enter our minds. That he may esteem, admire, and eventually imitate us need never occur to us. But without our realizing it, our life as a whole is a springboard into heaven for other people. Each separate good action is an individual rung of the ladder leading up to that springboard.

Bad example has an equal opposite effect on those who witness it. We do not have to intend to harm them spiritually. Independent of our intention, they are hurt spiritually by our bad conduct. Every act of vice, every commandment broken, every duty neglected is not just a nail in our own spiritual coffin. Each such act which our neighbor witnesses can also be a nail in his coffin.

Catholics can and should be apostles in both a negative and a positive way. They can and should lead others back to Christ or closer to Christ. In a negative way they can do this by leading a blameless life. Nothing in their conduct, nothing in their exterior life, must act as a stumbling block to those separated from Christ. This absence of bad example will cause others to think and reflect and compare themselves with the one whose life is blameless. They cannot help noticing such a one does not use the name of God and the Holy Name as if they were cheap, common words. Again they will observe that the smutty story or joke has no place in their conversation. Before long they note that the apostolic type of Catholic is silent about an absent neighbor when nothing good can be said of that person. Eventually they will observe that this type of Catholic makes no attempt to parade his virtues. Nor is he perpetually excusing his faults.

In a positive way an adult Catholic should be an apostle. Being one is difficult, if not impossible, unless a person has a thorough knowledge of his religion. We cannot lead others to Christ if he is a vague, misty figure whom we can barely recognize ourselves. His teaching we can impart only after that teaching has become a part of ourselves. Ignorance leads to argument, knowledge to explanation. About Christ and his teaching we cannot have too much explanation. Argument, no matter how little, will always be too much. Ignorance often results in calling a truth of religion a mystery, when it is not a mystery at all. There are certainly enough mysteries in religion without multiplying them unnecessarily. Of those which really exist, we should know what can be known about them. After all, "a mystery is not something about which we can know nothing; a mystery is something about which we cannot know everything."

3. No one gives what he does not possess. Before we can inspire others with a love for Christ, we must have a deep personal love for him ourselves. Before we can inspire their enthusiasm for the teaching of Christ, we must put into practice and exemplify that teaching in our own daily lives. A readiness to help others, to serve them, and to make sacrifices for them makes a far deeper impression than words and reasons. Willingness to undergo inconvenience, discomfort, and even downright suffering will convert people where the most forceful reasoning would fail.

The Catholic who says, "I am interested only in saving my own soul" is either weak or ignorant or bad. When God asked Cain about his brother Abel, Cain answered: "I don't know. Am I my brother's keeper?" Cain, as we know, was a murderer. In saying, "I am interested only in saving my own soul; I am not interested in the salvation of others," a Catholic would be using words different from those used by Cain. But his answer seems to imply a denial of any responsibility to be "his brother's keeper."

To be an apostle is to be "our brother's keeper." In society today we often face alternatives. Either we become our brother's keeper or, by our passivity and neglect, we become to him what Cain was to his brother Abel, his destroyer, his murderer.

VI. Thought for the Day

The privilege of a visit to Rome and to our Holy Father carries with it a responsibility. He has warned us that "the array of Christ's enemies grows ever more dangerously; the preachers of lying doctrine are ceaselessly at work" (*Humani Pontificatus*). The main task of all Catholics today is to reestablish the teachings and practice of the Christian religion in the family circle and throughout the whole of human society. No Catholic can be a good Catholic and be mediocre today. Since we have a social responsibility, we cannot ask how much must I do but rather how much can I do. Our task is to re-Christianize a de-Christianized world. This means that we must have an apostolic mentality. We must redeem and sanctify ourselves and all those with whom we come in contact.

VII. Concluding Prayer

"Memorare."

MARY'S KINDNESS

I. Introductory Prayer

II. Text

In the 4th chapter, the 32nd verse of his Epistle to the Ephesians, St. Paul exhorts us to "be kind to one another."

III. Setting

When the Blessed Virgin Mary heard from the angel Gabriel that her cousin Elizabeth was in her old age about to bear a child, she arose immediately and departed on her mission of kindness. Despite the fact that she had just received the announcement that she was to be the Mother of God, she went on what, for a young maiden, must have been an inconvenient, difficult journey of at least five day's duration. She passed through part of Galilee and hostile Samaria until she reached the mountains of Judea where Zechariah dwelt with his wife, Elizabeth. "Mary arose and went with haste into the hill country, to a town of Judah. And she entered the house of Zechariah and saluted Elizabeth. Now it came to pass, when Elizabeth heard the greeting of Mary, that the babe in her

107

womb leapt. And Elizabeth was filled with the Holy Spirit and cried out with a loud voice, saying, 'Blessed are you among women and blessed is the fruit of your womb. How have I deserved that the mother of my Lord should come to me? For behold, the moment that the sound of your greeting came to my ears, the baby in my womb leapt for joy. Yes, blessed is she who has believed that the things promised her by the Lord would be accomplished.' Mary said in reply, 'My soul magnifies the Lord and my spirit rejoices in God my Savior'" (Lk 1:39-47). In completing his description of Mary's visitation of kindness to Elizabeth, St. Luke adds the significant words: "and Mary remained with her about three months, then returned to her own home." The kindness of the Immaculate Heart of Mary was not satisfied with a brief visit. Her kindness had to do something extra. She remained for three months to assist and care for her cousin Elizabeth.

IV. Petition

O Lord, my God, do not let me forget to be kind.

V. Points of Meditation

1. The life of Jesus of Nazareth was a life of kindness. So also was the life of His Blessed Mother a life of kindness. When St. Peter gave an instruction to Cornelius, the Roman centurion, he spoke of Jesus Christ "who went about doing good" (Ac 10:38). Thus he summarizes the public life of our Lord principally in the words "he went about doing good." This has been called the condensed Gospel of St. Peter, the life of Christ in five words, the biography of personified kindness. We might also describe the life of Mary by saying that she went about doing good. St. Paul summed up the Incarnation in a similar way, when he wrote of the time "the goodness, and kindness of God, our Savior appeared" (Tt 3:4).

Since kindness was a predominant characteristic of the Sacred Heart of Jesus and of the Immaculate Heart of Mary, we might briefly meditate on its meaning. Father Faber tells us that "Kindness is the overflowing of self upon others. We put others in the place of self. We treat them as we should wish to be treated. We change places with them. For the time self is another and others are self." Kindness can also be described as the expansion of the charitable heart. St. Paul teaches that "charity is kind" (1 Cor 13:4). Charity is the very root and life of kindness. Kindness is true Christian charity in action. If we reflect on it, kindness is simply the outcome and exemplar of the divine precept, "You shall love your neighbor as yourself." The heart, if it would be kind, must overleap the boundaries of self. So we can rightly say that kindness is the expansion of the charitable heart; it is the overflowing of self upon others. Kindness has been described as "the foe of selfish coldness and gruffness and indifference; it is the music in the voice, the gentleness in the touch, the warmth in the grasp, the cheeriness of the glad welcome, the hushed accents of condolence." In short, kindness is the smile of all the virtues. It is the radiating goodness of the heart of charity.

2. We shall mutually profit by setting our thoughts on some traits of kindness as seen in Jesus and Mary. Kindness must not always wait — it must go about doing good. The Incarnation is the greatest of God's acts of kindness. "God so loved the world that he sent his only begotten Son." God was infinitely kind, when he emptied himself, came down to us, went about doing good, bringing the love of God to the hearts of mankind through a human heart. Our Lord was kind to the sick. The man, ill for 38 years, experienced the healing kindness of Christ when He said, "Arise, take up your bed and walk." The woman taken in adultery enjoyed the unique kindness of the Sacred Heart for sinners. We all know the story. Recall for a moment the conclusion of it and see the kindness of Christ. "'Woman, where are they who accused you? Has no one condemned you?' She said: 'No one, Lord.' And Jesus said: 'Neither will I condemn you. Go now and sin no more'"

(Jn 8:10-11). The name of Cana, the obscure village in Galilee, has not faded from the memory of Christian men and women for it reminds us of the kindness of Jesus and his Blessed Mother at the wedding feast. When Our Lady saw the wine failing and the immanent embarrassment of the bride's parents, the thought of a miracle to be worked by her Divine Son came at once to her mind. Without hesitation, she said to him, "They have no wine" (Jn 2:3). As we know, Jesus worked his first miracle, a miracle of kindness, anticipating his public life, at the prayer of his Blessed Mother.

Another trait of the kind heart is that it is easily approached. It repels no one. Was the way open to the Sacred Heart? Through the kindness of Jesus "the blind see, the lame walk, the lepers are made clean, the deaf hear, the dead rise again, to the poor the Gospel is preached" (Lk 7:22). The kindness of the Sacred Heart embraced all. "Come to me all you who labor and are heavily burdened and I will refresh you." Yet fearing that men would still hesitate to come to him, Jesus pictured himself as the Good Shepherd seeking the lost sheep of Israel. He is the Door of the Sheepfold, the Good Samaritan, the True Vine, the Way, the Truth and the Life accessible to all. In Our Blessed Mother's Litany of Loreto, her various titles of kindness tell us that the way is open for each and everyone of us to her Immaculate Heart. Mother Most Amiable, Virgin Most Merciful, Morning Star, Health of the Sick, Refuge of Sinners, Comforter of the Afflicted, Help of Christians, pray for us.

3. Kindness helps us to sanctify ourselves and all those with whom we come in contact. Nothing more effectively retards our spiritual growth than selfishness. Kindness is essentially un-selfish. If we wish to become unselfish there is one road open to us and that is the road of kindness. Every step along this road is a step heavenwards. Kindness also has the strange power of making us inwardly happy. In this atmosphere of happiness great things are done for God. Furthermore, we are reminded by Father Faber that "a proud man is seldom a kind man. Humility makes us kind and kindness makes us humble."

Kindness has the power of making the world happy. It is the office of kindness to constantly win souls back to God. Father Faber tells us that "Kindness has converted more sinners than either zeal, eloquence or learning; and these last three have never converted anyone unless they were kind also." Kindness, cooperating with God's grace, brings out the best that is in the character of others. Virtues that have been dormant for years come to life under its influence. Kindness reveals a man to himself. The greatest work that kindness does is that it makes the people, who are the objects of our kindness, kind themselves. Kindness is infectious. Since one leads to another, we can say that a kind act never dies.

VI. Thought for the Day

May we spend our lives in union with Jesus and Mary in an apostolate of kindness. May we realize that the Blessed Sacrament is a pledge not only of life and of Divine Love, but it is also a pledge of kindness. It is the kindness of God continuing to live among us.

VII. Concluding Prayer

"Memorare."

GOD'S MOTHER AND OURS

Feast of Mary's Divine Maternity
[This Feast is now celebrated
as a Solemnity on January 1]

I. Introductory Prayer

II. Text

"When Jesus, therefore, saw his mother and the disciple standing by, whom he loved, he said to his mother, 'Woman behold your son.' Then he said to the disciple, 'Behold your mother.'" These words are recorded in the Gospel of St. John the 19th chapter, 26th verse.

III. Setting

Jesus was dying. At the foot of the cross stood Mary, his sorrowful Mother, and John, his beloved disciple. The tender heart of our Savior was touched. He had given mankind his blood, his life. Yet he yearned to give more. What else remained for him to give? His dying eyes were turned to his Mother, Mary. His dying lips were opened to speak his last legacy of love. "Woman," he said, "Behold your son." And turning to John, "Son, behold your mother." In the Beloved Disciple, Jesus saw all mankind. At that moment Mary, the Mother of God, became the Mother of all men.

IV. Petition

Our prayer is that throughout our lives we may honor, love and imitate God's Mother and ours — the Blessed Virgin Mary. May the mystery of her Divine Maternity be the source of our true devotion to Mary!

V. Points of Meditation

1. Mary attended the execution of her son with heroism and courage. From the very beginning of his Passion, Mary had sorrowed with her Son. She had stood in Pilate's court; she had heard the "Ecce Homo" and the heart-breaking lashes; she beheld the crown of thorns piercing his head; she met him on the road to Calvary; she watched, she listened and she shuddered as the nails sank into his sacred hands and feet. She kept her watch beneath the cross and she seemed to feel each of his countless wounds in her own body. She was helpless! They made sport of her Son — the Son of God. They passed by shaking their fists and calling him vile names. She felt helpless because she could offer him no comfort.

Knowing that her son was truly the Son of God, possibly her thoughts went back over the years. Undoubtedly in her youth she had heard the prophetic words of Isaiah, "Behold, a virgin shall be with child, and bring forth a son, and they shall call his name Emmanuel, which being interpreted, is God with us" (Is 7:14). Now she recalled the wondrous words of the angel Gabriel at the time of the Annunciation. "The Holy Spirit shall come upon you, and the power of the Most High shall overshadow you. Therefore, the Holy One to be born shall be called the Son of God" (Lk 1:35). As soon as she gave her consent, the Second Person of the Blessed Trinity took a body and soul in her most chaste womb. Therefore, at the time of the Visitation, Elizabeth was inspired to exclaim, "How is it that the mother of my Lord should come to me?" (Lk 1:43).

On this feast of the Divine Maternity of Our Lady we might remind ourselves that Mary did not give to Christ his Divine Being. She gave to him his human nature. But that human nature is intimately united with his divine nature. Therefore, Mary can be called and is the Mother of God. Christ had two natures, the divine and the human. But Christ was only one Person, the divine. And this Divine Person is true man while he remained true God.

During the hours on Calvary's hill, possibly the Blessed Mother's thoughts went back to Bethlehem. What a difference between the crib and the cross! Then she could fold him warmly in her arms. She could kiss and caress him. Then there were shepherds and wise men. Now there were cruel soldiers and blasphemers.

In these circumstances, Jesus spoke as we have seen from the cross saying, "Woman, behold your Son." His heart was filled with compassion and sympathy for his Blessed Mother. He wished to offer her encouragement and consolation. He desired to give her someone who would care for her — who would be like a son to her. He was grateful for her countless sacrifices and he wished to provide for her. Although the words, "Behold your Son," were in one sense a consolation, at the same time it required a great act of charity on the part of the Blessed Mother to take as her sons the very people who were putting her Divine Son to death.

2. The words, "Behold your Mother," were addressed to St. John and through him to each and every one of us. He represented every man, woman and child who wishes to be called a Christian. At the foot of the cross, Mary is proclaimed the Mother of all of us — of the total Christ — of the Mystical Body. She is the Mother of Christ the Redeemer and the redeemed. She has given the whole

economy of our redemption a character of tenderness, of graciousness and of adaptation to the instinctive needs of human nature. Frequently, failure in the spiritual life can be traced to a want of appreciation of the indispensable role Mary, our Mother, plays in that life. She is the Mother of God and of all who are called to participate in the life of God. She is the Mother of Jesus and of the members of Jesus. We can measure our progress in perfection by the intensity of our devotion to her. With St. John, we accept the words of our Lord, "Behold your Mother" as a command as well as a consolation. St. John obeyed the command since the Gospel tells us that "from that hour the disciple took her into his home" (Jn 19:27). Like St. John we shall live in union with Mary so that through her we may always be with her Divine Son, Jesus Christ.

3. On this feast of the Divine Maternity, we should be mindful of the fact that all our devotion should hinge on the thought that Mary is our Mother and we should never doubt her love. We have seen ample proofs of her love during this pilgrimage. As the Mother of God, her intercession is all powerful. Am I tempted to sin? Mary will strengthen me to vanquish the tempter. Have I fallen? I must fly to my Mother. She will plead my cause. Am I discouraged in my efforts to grow in virtue? Mary will rouse my drooping spirits and obtain for me grace to make fresh endeavors. As true sons and daughters of Mary, we must honor, love and imitate her. We honor her by prayer — especially by praying the Rosary. We love her by placing her friendship above all human friendships. We imitate her by striving to acquire her virtues and "by forming Jesus Christ in our mortal flesh."

VI. Thought for the Day

All the mysteries of Our Lady's life, all the titles by which she is addressed, all the prerogatives which are hers and all the supernatural influence she exerts find their principle of synthesis in this one great truth which was solemnly enunciated at the

Council of Ephesus in the year 431: Mary is the Mother of God. We rejoice on this feast of her Divine Maternity which was established by Pope Pius XI in 1931. Echoing the words of the Holy Sacrifice of the Mass which we offer this morning, we pray, "Blessed is the womb of the Virgin Mary, which so loved the Son of the Eternal Father." Holy Mary, Mother of God and our Mother, pray for us.

VII. Concluding Prayer

"Memorare."

MARY'S SIMPLICITY

Feast of St. Francis Borgia

I. Introductory Prayer

II. Text

"Behold the handmaid of the Lord; let it be it done to me according to your word" (Lk 1:38).

II. Setting

Once again we contemplate the sacred scene of the Annunciation. When the angel Gabriel informed Mary that she was divinely chosen to be the mother of the Savior, the Son of God, the occasion certainly justified a speech. Mary's answer was a question and then an act of submission to the Divine Decree. She did not demand of Gabriel a proof that he was an ambassador from God and not a fallen spirit "transformed into an angel of light." She did not tell him in so many words that she had a vow of virginity and that his message placed her in a dilemma. To fulfill perfectly what she recognized as God's will was the aim and intention of her life. Her simplicity was wrapped up in that all pervading resolution. If virginity and maternity both were God's will, then the angel must have the solution to her dilemma. With this in mind, Mary questioned: "How shall this be, since I do not know man?" (Lk 1:34). Assured by Gabriel that all would be accomplished by the power of the Holy Spirit, Mary's answer was as simple as her question. "Behold the handmaid of the Lord; let it be done to me according to your word" (Lk 1:38).

IV. Petition

With the help of Our Lord and his Blessed Mother may we grow daily in the virtue of simplicity. This is the grace that we seek.

V. Points of Meditation

1. Any human virtue or perfection is but a dim reflection, a faint image of divine perfection. A human virtue shadows forth in an obscure manner a divine attribute. Of all God's perfections, perhaps the most inimitable is his simplicity. Yet in proportion to our ability and the graces we receive from God, we do have the obligation to imitate God's simplicity: "Be perfect as your heavenly Father is perfect" (Mt 5:48).

By nature God is simple, for he is not composed of parts and he is absolutely indivisible. We on the other hand, consist of bodies and souls. That is our nature. Evidently, since we cannot change our nature, our simplicity must consist in the way we think, intend, and act. We are as we will and St. Augustine says, "Men are so many wills."

All simplicity is not holy and spiritual. The devil is diabolically simple in that all his thoughts, intentions and actions are directed against God. A man of the world, especially a very successful man of the world, is often quite simple. In fact, he may

118

owe much, if not all, of his success to his simplicity. All his power, all his energy centers upon one big aim or objective in life. That objective may be money, power or reputation. Then there is a simplicity which we contemplate today and that is spiritual simplicity. In his book *The Imitation of Christ,* Thomas à Kempis tells us that "a man is raised up from the earth on two wings: simplicity and purity. There must be simplicity in his intention and purity in his desires" (Bk. 2, Chap. 4). Simplicity is a virtue that deals chiefly, if not exclusively with the intention.

When a person has a principal intention, when that intention aims at serving and pleasing God, when all his other intentions are subordinate to that principal and intention, and he employs all his power and all the means at his disposal to carry out his principal intention, then that person is simple. Our Lord, as Man, and Mary, his Mother, are perfect examples of simplicity in its highest form.

2. As man, Christ had one idea, one aim, one intention: to fulfill the will of God, his Father, even to the most minute detail. Time and time again in one form or another, he expresses this intention — this guiding objective of his life. "I do always the things which please him" (Jn 8:29). "My meat is to do the will of him who sent me that I may perfect his work" (Jn 4:34). "Not my will, but yours be done" (Lk 22:42). The Blessed Virgin Mary also exemplifies the virtue of simplicity in a singularly high degree. Our Lady, being wholly and utterly human, loved persons, and she also loved things. If her love for persons differed from ours, it was because she saw in people other creatures of God, made to his image and likeness, and to be loved for his sake. She never let her love for them degenerate to the point where she loved them predominantly, if not exclusively, for the good that they did to her. In speaking to God, St. Augustine said, "Too little does any man love you, who loves some other thing together with you, not loving it on account of you." Mary loved things and she saw in them, so many steppingstones reminding her of God and leading her back to God. They were his gifts to be valued, not primarily for themselves, but because they originated from God. "Better the love of

the Giver than the gift of the Lover." Thus in her love for things and for persons, the Blessed Virgin Mary was truly simple, always aiming at God and at the fulfillment of his will.

3. To what degree do we have the virtue of simplicity? To what extent do we make God the principal aim and objective of our lives? Cardinal Newman (*Plain and Parochial Sermons*) said, "The aim of most men esteemed, conscientious and religious... is to all appearances, not how to please God, but how to please themselves without displeasing him."

If we consider the way in which we spend our time, we shall find that it is divided into three unequal parts. One part we give to God, another part goes to our neighbor, while we keep the lion's share for ourselves. We go to Mass on Sunday, to confession once or twice a month, and to an occasional retreat, parish mission or novena. If we add to this the minutes that we spend saying morning and evening prayers, we give God just about 5% of an average week. We might say that we are too busy to do more — but the man who is too busy to pray *is too busy*. Much of our time is spent on our neighbor — but not for our neighbor or for God. Frequently, our neighbor is good to us, useful to us. We enjoy his company. Occasionally, a little spirituality creeps into this relationship and we realize that we should have the simple intention of fulfilling God's commandment of love of neighbor. In the time that we devote to ourselves, we have the general resolution not to violate the commandments of God in a serious matter. But along with this resolution, we seem to have a policy of doing without scruple whatever we can do without crime.

We shall cultivate this necessary virtue of simplicity by learning to esteem it. Simplicity helps us to achieve the purpose of life — to know, love and serve God and to be happy with him. In other words, we should have the simple intention of being saints — being friends of God. The first reason that we are here on earth is to adore God — to praise him. We praise him in our personal prayer — in the morning and in the evening — in offering Holy Mass with the priest. Although life in the world today has become more and more complex, we must keep our own personal interior life simple. Since the ABC of Christian living is to adore God first, as far as possible we must give a greater part of our time directly to his service. In this way we shall be imitating the simplicity of Our Lady as seen at Lourdes and at Fatima.

VI. Thought for the Day

In praying for the virtue of simplicity, we repeat the words of Our Lady, "Behold the handmaid of the Lord; let it be it done to me according to your word." We also reflect on the perfect expression of simplicity given to us by our Divine Teacher in the Lord's Prayer: "Thy will be done on earth as it is in heaven."

VII. Concluding Prayer

"Memorare."

MARY, CAUSE OF OUR JOY

OCTOBER 12TH
20th Sunday after Pentecost

I. Introductory Prayer
"Presence of God."

II. Text

As we offer the Holy Sacrifice of the Mass each morning with the priest we say, "I will go unto the altar of God, to God who gives joy to my youth" (Ps 42).

III. Setting

It has been historically established that the sailors of Christopher Columbus sang the "Salve Regina" — the "Hail Holy Queen" — as their small vessels made their long journey across the Atlantic Ocean. This hymn which has been chanted for centuries on every one of the five continents wherever Catholics come together, is a summary of Mary's claim to the title "Cause of Our Joy." She is indeed the cause of our joy because she is our life, our sweetness, and our hope to whom we turn, full of confidence, in this vale of tears. Pope Leo XIII was so devoted to this beautiful song of praise that he prescribed it to be said after every low Mass, in conjunction with other prayers, to secure Mary's intercession for the universal Church. The Blessed Virgin Mary is the cause of our joy because she gave Christ to the world. She is the Mother of God and our Mother and the Mediatrix of all graces.

IV. Petition

May Our Lady, the Cause of our Joy, fill our hearts with Christian optimism — with Christian joy.

V. Points of Meditation

1. In this morning's Gospel the ruler whose son was sick at Capernaum (Jn 4) manifested some admirable qualities. He had faith, humility, confidence and perseverance. "Jesus said to him: 'Go your way; your son lives.'" The man believed the word which Jesus said to him and went his way. As we know the Lord performed the miracle and at that same hour his son was healed. In addition to his other good qualities, the ruler was an optimist.

In comparing an optimist and a pessimist we might say that an optimist has a positive and constructive attitude towards life while a pessimist has a negative and destructive attitude. An optimist is a person who is filled with Christian joy, who keeps his sunny disposition going strong. We should keep in mind that there is a difference between a moderate optimist and an exaggerated optimist. To be an optimist is not to be a Pollyanna who covers all the realities of life with a sugar coating and refuses to realize that life has serious moments as all important things have. To be an optimist is not to turn away from sickness, suffering and death and to refuse to talk about such things because they are unpleasant. It is not optimism to be careless, to muddle through things somehow, and fondly believe that they will always turn out right. It is not optimism to let others make the effort and bear the burden of work and worry while we sit idly by and decide that all is well with the world.

Optimism that is genuine is made of a tougher fibre. Behind it rise courage, confidence, resolution. It is stripped of self, yet warm with the love of life and of those who live it; warm, most of all, with love for the Giver of life, whose goodness constitutes the fundamental goodness of life, whose beauty transforms and shines through creatures. The optimist is brave because he trusts in God, he is strong because he builds his viewpoint and his functioning upon Someone stronger than he, he is cheerful because he has faith which throws light upon all things, and because self casts no shadows over him. He is kind because joy of its very nature has a tendency to overflow and to communicate itself. This Christian joy which he has preserves and fosters his optimism and averts pessimism.

2. On the other hand, behind pessimism hides discouragement. Pessimism turns everything face downward, and ignores the best in people and things in order to find the worst. The pessimist is not kind and he is much too busy with his own gloomy reactions to be sympathetic with others. The pessimist allows the devil to have a holiday in his soul when he gives in to discouragement. There is a story told about the devil which illustrates this point. Once upon a time the devil decided to go out of business. He offered his tools for sale, arranged them attractively and labelled each with a price. They were a bad looking lot: Malice, Hatred, Envy, Jealousy, Sensuality, Deceit and all the other implements of evil. Apart from the rest lay a harmless-looking wedge-shaped tool, much worn, yet priced higher than any of the others. Someone asked the devil what it was. "That's Discouragement," was the reply. "Why do you have it priced so high?" "Because," replied the devil, "it is more useful to me than any of the others. I can pry open and get inside a man's conscience with that when I could not get near him with any of the others. And when once inside, I can use

him in whatever way suits me best. It is so worn because I use it with nearly everybody, since few people know that it belongs to me." We can help ourselves not to become discouraged by refraining from wasting vital forces by worrying over things that have gone amiss. Nothing is to be gained thereby. Discouragement paralyzes ability and self-confidence, destroys efficiency and curtails the effectiveness of every faculty. A doctor knows how discouragement can hamper the cure of a patient. It hides God's means and methods. It hides God himself.

3. This quality of optimism — joyfulness — is necessary for Christian living. St. Paul advises us, "Rejoice in the Lord always! Again, I say rejoice!" (Ph 4:4). The Psalmist advises, "Serve the Lord with gladness; come before him with joyful song" (Ps 100:2). Optimism which comes from joy illuminates, invigorates all our prayers, works and deeds. In other words, it is necessary to be of "good heart" to live the supernatural life successfully. It has been said that joyfulness is the essential characteristic of a saint. When we are joyful, we are peaceful, patient, gentle and serene. This disposition shines out of the eyes, lights up the face and puts music in the voice. In the life of Christ and his Blessed Mother, this spirit of Christian optimism, of joyfulness is radiant before us. Who can fathom the depth of the God-man's joy? There was no discouragement on Calvary. "Be of good heart," he said to the paralytic. Walking on the troubled waters, he spoke these consoling words, "Let not your heart be troubled, nor let it be afraid." We also have numerous examples of how joyfulness helped many of the saints in their pursuit of perfection such as St. Philip Neri, St. Francis, St. Thérèse, St. Pius X. We must work for a spirit of optimism and joy each day. We might well begin each day by saying, "This is the day which the Lord has made. We will rejoice and be glad in it" (Ps 1:18). In a certain sense we can make every day a joyful day *by willing it — by rejoicing in it.* Holy Mass, Holy Communion, Visits to the Blessed Sacrament, Our Lady's Rosary — these are special means of living in the state of grace which is a state of joy.

VI. Thought for the Day

As the Kingdom of God is within you so also the kingdom of joy is within you. Christian optimism and joy are to be found living in union with Mary, Our Mother in the presence of God. *Sursum Corda*, Lift up your hearts! "I will go unto the altar of God, to God who gives joy to my youth."

VII. Concluding Prayer

"Memorare."

MARY'S GRATITUDE

OCTOBER 13TH

I. Introductory Prayer

II. Text

"It is truly meet and just, right and availing unto salvation, that at all times and in all places we give thanks to you, O Holy Lord, Father Almighty, Everlasting God." These words are found in the Preface of the Holy Sacrifice of the Mass.

III. Setting

As Jesus of Nazareth was entering a certain town, he heard the cry: "Jesus, Master, have mercy on us." Never did a prayer come more from the heart than the piteous cry of those ten lepers. "Jesus, Master, have mercy on us." Their desire to be heard made them courteous and considerate. St. Luke adds the note that they "stood afar off." Not knowing the kindly Christ, they stood afar off lest he should be angry if they with their foul disease came too near him. The kindness of the Sacred Heart of Jesus manifested itself again on this occasion. He answered their prayers with the simple words, "Go show yourselves to the priests." The ten lepers set out to follow his instructions "And it came to pass as they went, they were made clean" (Lk 17:14). One of the lepers, a Samaritan, when he saw that he was made clean, his heart was filled with gratitude. His grateful heart struggled to find full expression of itself. He returned with a loud voice glorifying God. St. Luke tells us that he knelt in the presence of Jesus "giving thanks." His gratitude was an echo, a response to the kindness of the Sacred Heart..., yet Jesus was sadly surprised. "Were not ten made clean? Where then are the other nine? Did no one return to give glory to God except this foreigner?" (Lk 17:18). Today, the cry of the Sacred Heart is worded differently, yet it is still the same, "Behold the Heart that has loved men so much, even to suffering and death to show them its love, and in return, I receive for the most part nothing but ingratitude."

IV. Petition

With the help of the Blessed Mother, may the spirit of gratitude, the Christ-like spirit permeate our lives.

V. Points of Meditation

1. If anyone was asked to name one thing that seems to have fallen out of the religious practice of our fellowmen, it would be the duty of gratitude, the duty of thanksgiving. There is little enough prayer in the world today but there is still less of gratitude. Although we are driven to prayer by our own interests, it is love alone which leads us to acts of gratitude. "Thanks be to God! God be praised! Praised be Jesus Christ!" These are expressions of gratitude. They are simply attempts to put into words what every creature should feel when he sees the immensity of the debt that he owes to his Maker and his utter helplessness to repay him

except in grateful love. People forget.... They don't think, and so they are ungrateful.

Gratitude is the conscience of memory. Gratitude is the charitable heart's recognition of a debt. The grateful heart cheerfully and spontaneously admits that it owes much to the kindness of others. In our human weakness, we usually see more clearly what others fail to do for us than what they actually do. Gratitude is the echo of a charitable heart responding to the least favor. It is the vibration of the heartstrings in harmony with kindness shown. Gratitude compliments the acts of kindness bestowed on us. The grateful heart is the response to the kindly heart.

2. The Immaculate Heart of Mary is the best model of a grateful heart. At a very tender age she made the perfect response to God's love when she presented herself to live with God and for God in the Temple of Jerusalem. The gratitude of Mary is seen in this mystery of the Presentation as she offers herself promptly and entirely to God. "My beloved to me, and I to him" (Sg 2:16). In effect, Mary said, "I will live all his and die all his." Mary's life continued to be a life of thanksgiving. For example, her loving, grateful response to God's kindness was, "Be it done to me according to your word" and "My soul magnifies the Lord, and my spirit rejoices in God my Savior" (Lk 1:38-46). Mary's Son, Jesus Christ, possessed the most grateful of all created hearts because to infinite favors it made a perfect response. At the most solemn moments of his life, Christ voices his ever abiding gratitude to the Father. Standing before the tomb of Lazarus, Jesus, lifting up his eyes, said, "Father I give you thanks that you have heard me" (Jn 11:41). On the occasion of the miracle of the feeding of the five thousand, the kindly, grateful heart of Jesus revealed itself. "And taking the seven loaves, giving thanks, he broke and gave to his disciples to set before them" (Mk 8:6). It has been said that the Incarnation was a great act of Divine kindness to us. The Incarnation was even a greater act of kindness to the human nature of Christ, which was lifted to a sublime height. Many virtuous motives have been advanced as to why Christ accepted and

endured his passion. St. Paul frequently advanced the virtue of Charity as the motive. "He loved and delivered himself up for me." We may look on the Passion as the loving response made by Christ to the favor of the Incarnation. But what is gratitude if it is not love's reply to kindness received. Thus, we arrive at the beautiful concept that the "Passion was an act of thanksgiving for the Incarnation." The Heart of Jesus Christ was a grateful Heart. It was gratitude itself.

3. Let us recall a few reasons why we should be grateful. In the life of each one of us, there has been a special and personal revelation of Divine Love. This special and personal revelation of Divine Love is seen in the fatherly providence that has watched over the lives of each one of us. What an immense chain of Divine graces extends from the present hour on your voyage home to the hour of your baptism and mine. How tireless has been God's love for us. Consider the way in which things have been arranged for our happiness. How the obstacles have disappeared as we drew nearer to them and just when they looked insurmountable. How temptations have turned to our well being. Very often, what seemed to be chastisements when we faced them changed to acts of Divine Love when we looked back on them. Thanks be to God for his boundless charity by which he first created the world, then redeemed it and after that prepared us for eternal glory! Thanks be to God for the gift of faith and for all the supernatural wonders of our holy religion! Thanks be to God for the adorable sacrifice of the Mass and the personal presence of Jesus in the Blessed Sacrament of the altar! Thanks be to God for the privilege, joys and sorrows of this pilgrimage with his Eminence, our Cardinal Spellman! Thanks be to God for the opportunity that we have had to be in Lourdes, Fatima and the Eternal City with him!

If we cultivate this spirit of gratitude, we truly shall have the spirit of the saints. In one of the revelations of St. Catherine of Siena, God the Father tells her that thanksgiving makes the soul incessantly delight in him so that it frees it from negligence and lukewarmness. The heart of St. Paul was filled with gratitude.

Most of his letters began with the giving of thanks. "I give thanks to my God always" (Phm 4). St. Bernard advises, "Speak to God in thanksgiving and you will get graces more and more abundantly." In our relationships with others, the spirit of gratitude like the spirit of kindness is contagious. A simple "thank you" will often open the hardest heart and bring out the best that is in the character of others. May this spirit of thanksgiving, this Eucharistic spirit, this Christlike spirit permeate our whole lives.

VI. Thought for the Day

As we offer the Holy Sacrifice of the Mass this morning we beseech our Lord and his Blessed Mother to give us a grateful spirit. Personally, I wish to thank all of you by using the words of St. Paul, "I give thanks to my God in all my remembrance of you, always in all my prayers making supplication for you all with joy" (Ph 1:34). To His Eminence, who is with us in spirit, we might all say in the words of St. Paul, "We give thanks to God always for you, continually making a remembrance of you in our prayers; being mindful before God our Father of your work of faith, and labor and charity and your enduring hope in our Lord Jesus Christ" (1 Th 1:2-3).

VII. Concluding Prayer

"Memorare."

Prayer After Meditation

The "Memorare"

Remember, O Most gracious Virgin Mary that never was it known that any one who fled to your protection, implored your help, or sought your intercession, was left unaided. Inspired with this confidence, I fly unto you, O Virgin of virgins, my Mother; to you do I come, before you I stand, sinful and sorrowful; O Mother of the Word Incarnate, despise not my petition, but in your mercy hear and answer me. Amen.

(An Indulgence of 3 years. A plenary indulgence once a month on the usual conditions for the daily recitation of this prayer.)